THE
GREATER
COMMUNITY

A BOOK OF THE
NEW MESSAGE
FROM GOD

THE
GREATER
COMMUNITY

CONTACT
with Intelligent Life
in the Universe

AS REVEALED TO
Marshall Vian Summers

THE
GREATER
COMMUNITY

Edited by Darlene Mitchell
Cover and interior: Designed by Reed Summers
ISBN: 978-1-942293-40-8
NKL POD Version 7.0
Library of Congress Control Number: 2017901448

Publisher's Cataloging-in-Publication
(Provided by Quality Books, Inc.)

Summers, Marshall Vian, author.
　　The Greater Community : contact with intelligent life in the
　　universe / as revealed to
Marshall Vian Summers.
　　pages cm
　　"A book of the New Message from God."
　　LCCN 2017901448
　　ISBN 978-1-942293-40-8
　　ISBN 978-1-942293-41-5 (ebook)

　　1. Society for the New Message--Doctrines.
　　2. Spiritual life--Society for the New Message.
　　3. Extraterrestrial beings.　4. Civilization--
　　Extraterrestrial influences.　5. Human-alien encounter
　　6. Cosmology.　I. Society for the New Message.
　　II. Title.

BP605.S58S825 2017　　　　　　299'.93
　　　　　　　　　　　　　QBI17-900021

The Greater Community is a book of the New Message from God and is published by New Knowledge Library, the publishing imprint of The Society for the New Message. The Society is a religious non-profit organization dedicated to presenting and teaching a New Message for humanity. The books of New Knowledge Library can be ordered at www.newknowledgelibrary.org, your local bookstore and at many other online retailers.

The New Message is being studied in more than 20 languages in over 90 countries. *The Greater Community* is being translated into the many languages of our world by a dedicated group of volunteer student translators from around the world. These translations will all be available online at www.newmessage.org.

The Society for the New Message
P.O. Box 1724　Boulder, CO 80306-1724
(303) 938-8401　(800) 938-3891
011 303 938 84 01 (International)　(303) 938-1214 (fax)
newmessage.org　newknowledgelibrary.org
email: society@newmessage.org

Go out on a clear night and look up.

———————

Your destiny is there.

———————

Your difficulties are there.

———————

Your opportunities are there.

———————

Your redemption is there.

From *Greater Community Spirituality*
Chapter 15: Who Serves Humanity?

THE
GREATER
COMMUNITY

TABLE OF CONTENTS

INTRODUCTION

The Greater Community is a book of Revelation given by
the Creator of all life to the human family through the Messenger
Marshall Vian Summers.

In this book of Revelation, God is throwing open the doors to
the universe of intelligent life in which our world has always existed.
Here God is revealing to humanity the "Greater Community" of
worlds in which we live and with this our destiny to emerge out of
our isolation in the universe as a free and self-determined race. Only
God could provide a Revelation such as this. Only God could give
humanity a true and clear picture of life in the universe, for God is
the Author of all life in the universe.

This book contains revelations about life in the universe
never presented to humanity before. Here God is preparing us
for the realities, the challenges and the opportunities of engaging
with life on a larger scale. With this is presented the awareness and
education we will need to protect our freedom and sovereignty, and
to contribute the spiritual gifts of our world in a larger community
of life in the universe.

Only a Revelation from the Creator of all life could bring this
to you. Throughout human history, the Creator has given successive
Revelations to meet the growing needs of people and nations at great
turning points in the evolution of humanity. Through the Prophets,
Messengers and revealed Teachings of the past, God's Revelations
have entered the world at specific times to advance human awareness
and awaken humanity to the needs and opportunities of that time
and the times to come.

However, none of God's previous Revelations could prepare
us for the reality of the Greater Community and reveal the meaning
and destiny of human spirituality within this larger context of life.
Humanity simply had not progressed that far in ancient times.
The tribes and nations of the world had not yet developed into

an international community capable of world awareness and communication. The world had been visited on a small scale in ancient times, but nothing like the scale of contact underway today. Humanity had not yet arrived at the threshold of emerging into a Greater Community of life in the universe.

Now that threshold has come, and the process of Revelation is continuing anew through a New Message from God, of which *The Greater Community* is but a small part. The words of this text are a direct communication from God, translated into human language by the Angelic Presence that watches over this world, and then spoken through the Messenger Marshall Vian Summers, who has given over 30 years of his life to this process of Revelation.

Though it appears to be a book in the hand, *The Greater Community* is something far greater. This is a book of original Revelation from God given to prepare each person for the next chapter in the development and evolution of the human family. This Revelation holds a key to the future and well-being of every person on Earth.

The Greater Community is the fourth book of Volume 1 of the New Message from God. *The Greater Community* contains 11 individual revelations, each given at different times and places and compiled by the Messenger into this text.

The Greater Community presents an expansive vision of the universe in which we live. Here God reveals what awaits humanity in the universe at large, the challenge and complexity of interaction between worlds, and the essential tools humanity will need to navigate its engagement with forces from beyond our world. Here the human family eclipses its millennia-old isolation in the universe and learns to interact wisely with other forms of intelligent life. This interaction will greatly expand how we view ourselves, God and our place in the universe.

Our world is emerging into a Greater Community of intelligent life. Contact has begun, and our isolation in the universe is now coming to an end. Yet this is not contact of a beneficial and benign nature. This is an Intervention into human affairs that threatens to undermine our freedom and survival as a race. This is the greatest event in human history. It is happening now, yet we are unaware and unprepared.

Contact has begun at a time when we are racing towards a dangerous and uncertain future in our world. Humanity is outstripping the Earth of its life-giving resources at an alarming rate, changing the climate of the world, and degrading and destroying the natural environment as never before. At the same time, political, social and religious conflict and division are escalating, fracturing the human family when instead we must be working to find a stable and functioning unity to ensure our collective survival. We are fractured and divided and this makes us vulnerable to outside influence and intervention from the universe around us.

The Greater Community emphasizes that humanity has reached a critical threshold in its evolution, a time of convergence when the reality of a changing world and the reality of Intervention from the universe collide. The revelations contained in this book teach how these two realities are connected, what this time of convergence and collision will mean for us and how we can prepare to navigate this new and challenging future.

We now stand at a juncture where we must make a fundamental choice: Do we work together for the safety and survival of the human race and perhaps the future of all life on Earth and, with this, prepare for the reality of contact? Or do we plunge deeper into the chaos of competition, division and war, making our world ever more vulnerable to Intervention from beyond and obscuring and denying the clear truth that we are one humanity with one destiny in the universe? This is a choice not only for leaders and governments, but for every person on Earth. This choice will determine not only our survival in the world, but within the Greater Community of worlds as well.

The Greater Community reveals that alien forces from beyond the world have been operating in our midst for many years. These forces do not represent a friendly visitation but instead a dangerous Intervention with an agenda to gain access to the Earth and its resources. This Intervention seeks to take advantage of the vulnerabilities of the human family, undermining our fragile trust in one another, demeaning our faith in human leadership, and exacerbating the divisions and long-standing conflicts between nations and religions. At a time of great internal change in the world, this Intervention poses the greatest threat to humanity's freedom and sovereignty we have ever faced.

The arrival of dangerous forces from beyond our world signals that our destined emergence into a Greater Community of worlds has begun. Our isolation in the universe is over. Like the natives of the New World centuries ago, discovered by colonial powers eager for wealth, resources and advantage, we have been discovered. Now we are all the natives of the "new world" and must deal with intervening forces from beyond our world. We are unprepared. And yet now the preparation has been given, given through the power of Revelation from the Creator of all life.

Though challenging, this presents the greatest opportunity for humanity to outgrow its destructive and primitive tendencies and finally establish a level of cooperation, stability and security never before achieved. The revelations contained in *The Greater Community* teach that it is the convergence of the Great Waves of environmental, social and political change in our world along with humanity's emergence into the Greater Community that create the most powerful opportunity to unite the human family—the most powerful opportunity we will ever have to finally bring an end to war and the destruction of our natural environment. This will be achieved not through high idealism, but out of sheer necessity, for this is a requirement for freedom and survival in the Greater Community.

INTRODUCTION

In facing a non-human universe and the Intervention that is operating in our world, we can see that our differences as humans are small. Here we can go beyond the political, religious and ethnic lines that have divided us in the past in order to protect our future and freedom as a human family, which are now being threatened from beyond. Finally, the disparate groups and factions of the human family can come to the table, recognizing the necessity of stewarding the Earth, its environment and its resources, and securing this Earth as our one home in a Greater Community of worlds. All of this becomes a natural desire and a natural direction when we adopt a Greater Community awareness, an awareness that accounts for life beyond our world. The power of this greater awareness to resolve the problems of our world today should not be underestimated.

The Greater Community presents the reality of Knowledge, the spiritual intelligence that lives within each person. This Knowledge is native to us and, once developed and brought forth, will naturally move through us to address the growing problems of our world. It is Knowledge that will enable us to correctly discern the alien Intervention in our world along with its intentions and its activities. Here Knowledge is the source of our innate ability to see and know the truth beyond any force of deception or manipulation. This is a critical strength that humanity must develop if it is to safely and wisely engage with powerful forces from beyond the world.

In addition to the revelation on Knowledge, *The Greater Community* presents Wisdom from the Greater Community itself. Here God is connecting humanity to those races who have passed through the evolutionary challenges we are going through now to cultivate and express a greater spiritual awareness and ability in their worlds. These races have the potential to become the Allies of Humanity and have been called by God to provide an education and perspective to prepare our young and emerging race. For the first time in history, a New Revelation from God is being accompanied by a gift of wisdom and relationship from those in the universe who are allied with God's work in the Greater Community and support humanity's emergence as a free and self-determined race. By coming to understand the wisdom of the Allies of Humanity (learn more at www.alliesofhumanity.org), we come to see our innate inclusion within a larger community of life and the greater process of development and spiritual evolution our world is called to undertake.

While *The Greater Community* speaks on the Allies of Humanity, it also warns us of an Intervention in our world: the arrival of dangerous and predatory races from the Greater Community, commercial forces who seek to gain access to our world, its resources and its people. Here God is sounding a warning to humanity. This encounter has the power to undermine human civilization and destroy human freedom. Yet this threat also presents the necessity for human unity and the end of human conflict. This is the power of the coming of the Greater Community. It is for this reason that God has spoken again to provide a Revelation of warning, blessing and preparation for our world.

Contact with intelligent life in the universe is a world event like no other. It is the next great step in the development and evolution of the human family. It is unstoppable. It is inevitable. It is happening now. Here we must choose to either undertake the preparation and education for the Greater Community and, in so doing, ensure the freedom and sovereignty of our world, or continue to fight and struggle with each other, blind to our common future and blind to the Intervention now present in the world. It comes down to the decision of each person: the decision to be aware or to be unaware, the decision to prepare or to be blind to a future now racing towards us.

Remarkably, you are in the world at this time. You are coming to learn about humanity's emergence into the Greater Community, and you have found this book, a book of Revelation from the Creator of all life. It is no coincidence that this is the case. We each have been sent into the world at this time to serve the needs of our time and of a world in transition. Indeed, some in the world today have a Greater Community connection and lineage that extends beyond this life alone.

The revelations of *The Greater Community* have been given to activate this awareness in you, to call forth the deeper Knowledge that you carry, and to provide you with the education and preparation you will need to be a contributor to an emerging world. In time, this will bring true clarity, inner certainty and direction to your life, for now you are moving with the greater movement of the world itself.

Now you can gain a greater understanding of the true context for your life and the mysterious and perhaps inexplicable calling that has brought you to this point. This understanding will naturally call forth the gifts you carry, the gifts you brought with you from your Ancient Home to serve the world at this time.

The door to the Greater Community is opening now. Never before has this door opened to the human family. Now it is time to pass through this threshold and prepare for a greater life in a greater universe of worlds.

The Society for the New Message

ABOUT THE NEW MESSAGE
FROM GOD

---

*T*he New Message from God is a living communication from the Creator of all life to the heart of every man, woman and child on Earth. This communication is here to ignite the spiritual power of humanity, to sound God's Calling for unity amongst the world's nations and religions, and to prepare humanity for a radically changing world and for its destiny in a larger universe of intelligent life.

The New Message from God is the largest Revelation ever given to humanity, given now to a literate world of global communication and growing global awareness. It is not given for one tribe, one nation or one religion alone, but instead to reach the entire world, a world very different from the ancient world of the former Messengers. Never before has there been a Divine Revelation of this depth and magnitude, given by God to all people of the world in the lifetime of the Messenger.

The New Message from God has not entered the world through the existing religious authorities and institutions of today. It has not come to the leaders of religion or to those who garner fame and recognition.

Instead, God's New Message has entered the world as it has always done. It has come quietly, unlooked for and unannounced, given to a humble man chosen and sent into the world for this one task, to be a Messenger for humanity at this great turning point.

At the center of the New Message from God is the original Voice of Revelation, which has spoken the words of every book of the New Message. Never before has the Voice of Revelation, the Voice that spoke to the Messengers and Prophets of the past, been recorded in its original purity and made available to each person to hear and to experience for themselves. In this way, the Word and the Sound of Revelation are moving in the world again.

In this remarkable process of spoken Revelation, the Presence of God communicates beyond words to the Angelic Assembly that oversees the world. The Assembly then translates this communication into human language and speaks all as one through their Messenger, whose voice becomes the vehicle for this greater Voice—the Voice of Revelation.

The words of this Voice were recorded in audio form, transcribed and are now made available in the books of the New Message. In this way, the purity of God's original spoken Message is preserved and given to all people in the world.

The Messenger has walked a long and difficult road to bring the New Message from God to you and to the world. The process of Revelation began in 1982 and continues to this day.

At this time, the Messenger is engaged in compiling over three decades of spoken Revelation into a final and complete testament— The One Book of the New Message from God. This new testament will be divided into six volumes and possibly more. Each volume will contain two or more books, and each book will be organized into chapters and verses. Therefore, the New Message from God will be structured in the following way: Volume > Book > Chapter > Verse.

In order to bring this spoken communication into written form, slight textual and grammatical adjustments were made by the Messenger. This was requested of him by the Angelic Assembly to aid the understanding of the reader and to convey the Message according to the grammatical standards of the written English language.

In some instances, the Messenger has inserted a word not originally spoken in the Revelation. When present, you will often find this inserted word in brackets. Consider these bracketed insertions as direct clarifications by the Messenger, placed in the text by him alone in order to ensure that ambiguities in the spoken communication do not cause confusion or incorrect interpretations of the text.

In some cases, the Messenger has removed or changed a word to aid the readability of the text. This was usually done in the case of certain conjunctions, articles, pronouns and prepositions that made the text awkward or grammatically incorrect.

The Messenger alone has made these slight changes and only to convey the original spoken communication with the greatest clarity possible. None of the original meaning or intention of the communication has been altered.

The text of this book has been structured by the Messenger into verse. Each verse roughly signals the beginning or ending of a distinct topic or message point communicated by the Source.

The verse structure of the text allows the reader to access the richness of the content and those subtle messages that may otherwise be missed in longer paragraphs of text that convey multiple topics. In this way, each topic and idea communicated by the Source is given its own standing, allowing it to speak from the page directly to the reader. The Messenger has determined that structuring the text in verse is the most efficacious and faithful way of rendering the original spoken revelations of the New Message.

The rendering of this text is according to the Messenger's original will and intention. Here we are privileged to witness the process of preparation and compilation being undertaken by the Messenger, in his own time, by his own hands. This stands in stark contrast to the fact that the former great traditions were largely not put into written form by their Messengers, leaving the original Revelation vulnerable to alteration and corruption over time.

Here the Messenger seals in purity the texts of God's New Message and gives them to you, to the world and to all people in the future. Whether this book is opened today or 500 years from now, God's original communication will speak from these pages with the same intimacy, purity and power as on the day it was spoken.

CHAPTER 1

HUMANITY'S EMERGENCE INTO THE GREATER COMMUNITY

As revealed to
Marshall Vian Summers
on July 18, 2008
in Boulder, Colorado

Humanity stands at the threshold of space, at the threshold of a Greater Community of intelligent life in the universe. Though there are great problems here in the world, and though humanity is facing the Great Waves of change that are coming to the world— environmental deterioration; diminishing resources; growing economic and political instability and the risk of competition, conflict and war—humanity has reached a great threshold in its evolution. It has reached a point of no return regarding its position within this Greater Community of intelligent life.

Your isolation in the universe is over. From this point on, you will have to contend with various forces coming to the world, seeking to gain advantage here.

You live in a beautiful world with magnificent natural resources. But your world exists in a well-inhabited part of space where there are many powerful technological societies who have established complex networks of trade.

These societies, like so many others in the Greater Community, have outstripped their worlds' natural resources and must now engage in a very complex arrangement of trade and commerce to gain access to the very resources that they need. Their technological advancement has not freed them from this need, but has indeed escalated the requirements of life.

There are free societies within your region of space who are not part of these complex networks of trade, who have been able to maintain individual freedom and self-determination for their peoples.

You are emerging into a complex set of circumstances. It is very unlike what most people think or speculate about regarding the possibilities of intelligent life in the universe.

Many people believe the universe is a great empty place, and if life does exist, it is rare. Many people think that if humanity were to encounter another race of beings in the universe, this race of beings would be inordinately interested in humanity, and would want to help humanity and share their wisdom and technology with this young emerging race in the world.

But, alas, the situation is very different. You are emerging into a very competitive environment where war and conflict are rare, but where the forces of influence and manipulation are powerful. You are emerging into a set of circumstances that are well established, and have been established for a very long time.

For eventually, races in the universe seek to establish stability above all else, and this stability requires the establishment of strong relations in trade with other nations so that their competition then ceases to be destructive. Advanced technology requires many resources, and the access to these resources must be secured. So very longstanding arrangements are made, and very little deviation or rebellion within these networks is tolerated.

HUMANITY'S EMERGENCE INTO THE GREATER COMMUNITY

It is as if humanity were a little child coming out of its house for the first time and recognizing it lives in a big city controlled by powerful forces that the little child cannot understand. It is very different from the storybooks the child would have read or from the child's imagination. It is not a wonderful place where everyone is happy and everyone is supported and everyone gets along really well.

The larger neighborhood of life into which you will emerge and the forces that you may encounter there, are not inordinately interested in humanity. They do not share humanity's values. They are not human or even human-like in most cases. But they do share the difficulties of living within a physical reality—the difficulties of security and securing resources, the difficulties of competition and all of the inherent problems that civilization poses despite its many benefits.

Like everyone in the Greater Community, you must face the boundaries that life and nature create. Technology cannot surmount most of these. Thus, everyone is facing the problems of survival and security, competition and so forth.

Humanity is a very young race. It is infatuated with technology. It thinks it is inordinately important in the universe. It believes and assumes its values and its aspirations are universal. This is understandable, of course, because humanity has never had to compete and survive within this Greater Community of life. Isolated within your own world, unable to travel abroad, you are, of course, ignorant of the realities of life within this far greater arena.

It is to educate humanity about the reality and the spirituality of the Greater Community that represents one of the primary purposes for the New Message that has been sent into the world from the Creator of all life. For only God knows what is really happening in the Greater Community and how humanity must prepare itself even for the Great

Waves of change that are coming to the world and that are upon you now.

The connection between the Great Waves of change and humanity's emergence into this Greater Community of intelligent life is very significant. As is the case in the evolution of so many societies in the universe, humanity is now outstripping its world's natural resources. This brings you to a great threshold.

First, it invites intervention by races who want to secure those biological resources for themselves. They will use all means necessary to gain this access, though force in this case is rarely employed.

You have also reached the threshold where humanity will have to choose—even consciously choose—whether it will fight and struggle over these remaining resources in the world or whether it will unite to preserve them and to secure them and to attain a stable environment for the future.

It is at this point that so many worlds are contacted from others who offer them technology and resources. If the native peoples have exhausted their own world's ability to sustain them, they will have to accept these offers. But it is these offers that will rob the native peoples of their self-determination, their freedom and their self-sufficiency.

For once you become reliant upon networks of trade in the universe, it is these networks that will determine how you will live and what you will do. Their influence over you will be inordinate because they will be controlling resources that are essential for your survival and well-being, and you must rely upon them.

HUMANITY'S EMERGENCE INTO THE GREATER COMMUNITY

It is the problem of losing one's self-sufficiency and becoming dependent upon others. If humanity is to become a free and self-determined race in the universe, which represents your greater destiny, you must not lose your self-sufficiency within this larger environment.

For there are three requirements for a race to be free in the universe, and especially in the regions that are well inhabited where networks of trade have been well established. You must be united, you must be self-sufficient and you must be extremely discreet.

At present, humanity is not united and is at risk of becoming ever more fractured and contentious, facing a world of declining resources.

You are losing your self-sufficiency with each passing day as you deplete the abundance of this world, as you overspend your natural inheritance, as you recklessly drive into the future, wanting to consume ever more from a world of finite resources.

You are hardly discreet, since you are broadcasting your strengths and weaknesses out into the universe for everyone to see. This, of course, threatens your future and threatens the possibility of your securing freedom in the future within this larger arena of life, where freedom itself is rare.

Large technological societies are often very secular in nature. They do not allow for individual expression. They do not honor the reality and the presence of the Creator of all life. The state has become their religion, and stability is maintained through a very strict hierarchy of structure.

This is the case in nations that rely upon one another for resources. They become ever more like one another, even though they are still distinct societies. They are forced to conform to a certain degree because of their interdependence.

That is why free nations in regions of space such as the one in which your world exists remain largely self-sufficient or will only trade to a limited degree with one another. They will seek to be very discreet, for free societies in the universe do not coexist well with those that are not [free].

This education about the Greater Community is essential, for you must have a sense of what you are preparing for, and you must begin to realize your own responsibilities here on Earth. You are emerging into a larger arena of life. It is not an arena that you will control or even influence to any degree whatsoever. You are emerging out of isolation.

Races from the Greater Community are already here interfering in human affairs—seeking to establish themselves as centers of power and influence here, operating secretly behind the scenes, influencing people in positions of power, taking citizens against their will, functioning in ways that are highly dangerous and hazardous for the human family.

Yet people go about life as if nothing is happening, consumed with their own needs, consumed with human conflict and corruption, consumed with the difficulties of life here in this one world, unaware and unconcerned about the presence of an Intervention here. Those few people who are aware of this presence are being persuaded to perceive it as beneficial, as benign and, in some cases, as even representing salvation for the human family.

HUMANITY'S EMERGENCE INTO THE GREATER COMMUNITY

Facing a world of declining resources and growing instability, humanity is particularly vulnerable to persuasion and intervention. There are many reasons for this. But the reality is that humanity is facing its greatest challenge from the outside and is not responding.

There are individuals and governments within your world who are aware of this, of course, but the public at large has no notion of the hazards that it is now facing at its borders to space. These are hazards that humanity can face and overcome, but you must unite and become educated for this to be possible.

Those races who are here in the world today are relying entirely upon human acquiescence and submission. They are not using force to achieve their goals. If humanity does not give this permission, does not acquiesce and does not submit, then these forces must withdraw.

The New Message for humanity explains why this is the case, but this will require you to study this and to become educated about the reality of life beyond your borders. You cannot make wild assumptions or hold to old ideas or opinions and have any hope of gaining this education and this understanding. For how could you know? How could anyone in the world know what is happening in the Greater Community of life around you?

This must be provided to you from a greater Revelation. While you have Allies in the universe who have sent you their Briefings, their wisdom and their recommendations, truly this Revelation must come from the Creator of all life. This Revelation must come for humanity's well-being. It was never needed in the world before, but it is needed now.

Humanity cannot prepare itself for a Greater Community that it cannot understand. It cannot prepare itself for a set of circumstances that it cannot witness. Yet this preparation is vitally needed in the world today.

You have great barriers and great walls between your nations. You have built up immense defensive and offensive capabilities between your nations. But you have your backs to the universe. You are not paying attention. You are not bringing wisdom to bear here—learning the lessons of intervention from your own history, realizing that this competition is part of nature, and the universe represents nature on a greater and almost incomprehensible scale.

The Creator of all life has given you Knowledge, a deeper intelligence within you. It represents your ability to realize the truth beyond any deception, beyond any preference, beyond hope, beyond fear, beyond all of the many things that cloud humanity's vision and understanding.

You have come into the world to serve the world under these very circumstances. You are not here by accident. What has really brought you into the world is connected to humanity's emergence into the Greater Community and to the great difficulties that humanity will face here on Earth as the result of its misuse and overuse of the world.

This represents the big picture of your life. It represents the reality of humanity's existence and the great threshold that humanity is now facing. Yet who is thinking of these things? Who can see clearly here? Who can bring common sense to an entirely different and new set of circumstances? Who has the objectivity to face challenges of this nature without projecting their own fears, preferences and denial upon it?

Humanity at this moment can barely even face its own difficulties here on Earth with any degree of clarity and vision. How will it face a Greater Community of life? Where will it find the strength to unite in the face of this Greater Community and to establish itself as a free and self-determined race within this larger arena of life?

These are questions that you really cannot answer, for you need the Power and the Grace of the Creator of all life to instruct you and to prepare you. You cannot prepare yourself. You do not even know what you are preparing for, or what the preparation will require and how you will be able to achieve a greater stability in the world and preserve the world's resources so that your freedom in the future may have a foundation here.

People will lose hope in the face of the Great Waves of change. They will lose hope and self-confidence in the face of the Greater Community. They will lose hope, not because they do not have the strength, but because they do not realize they have the strength to face these great and formidable obstacles that all races in life will encounter sooner or later.

Humanity has the possibility for Self-Knowledge. It has the awareness of the Creator of all life sufficiently to call upon a greater inner strength. It has learned the lessons of nature sufficiently within this world to bring this wisdom to bear in its encounter with a Greater Community of life.

But there are things that humanity cannot see and cannot know regarding what life is like beyond its borders—what this Greater Community is really like, how it functions and how a race such as your own must approach this [reality] in order to secure your freedom and sovereignty within this world.

You do not know yet your opportunities here and the dangers that surround them. No one in the world is educated about the Greater

Community. If you were, you would be responding very differently to the presence of foreign powers in your midst. This would become a worldwide focus, and the emphasis would be on establishing your own rules of engagement with whomever you are encountering now and will likely encounter in the future.

You would end your wars and your conflicts, realizing how vulnerable they make you to outside influence and manipulation. You would bring a greater sobriety and objectivity to bear in discerning those presences who are in the world and in counteracting their behavior here. You would realize that everything that you have is at risk now—all that humanity has achieved that is beneficial, all that humanity has created is at risk now.

You are facing a set of influences that seek not to destroy you, but to use you, to employ you in service to them. It is time to end your ceaseless conflicts and to prepare to engage with the Greater Community of intelligent life. This is far more important than any issues of contention you have with one another. Your divisions, your competition, your conflicts and your unwillingness to support one another between your nations, only make you weak and vulnerable in the face of this Greater Community.

Your few Allies in the universe who are aware of your existence, those races that live in your neighborhood of space who have achieved a degree of self-sufficiency and self-determination, have sent you a set of Briefings to warn you of the foreign presences who are in the world today and to help prepare you for the realities of life within the Greater Community itself.

Their testimony was called for by the Creator of all life, for humanity must know that it has possible friends in the universe. They are not in the world today. They are not interfering in human affairs. They

are watching you from afar. They know that the real preparation
must come from the Creator of all life, for only the Creator of all life
knows everything about the Greater Community and everything that
humanity will need to know, to do and to not do to prepare for this
Greater Community.

The Creator of all life has brought you Knowledge and Wisdom from
this Greater Community and has sent a warning, a blessing and a
preparation into the world. It is here to prepare humanity for the
greatest event in human history, the greatest threat to human freedom
and self-determination and the greatest opportunity for human unity
and cooperation.

Why would any nation in the world fight with other nations here if
they realized that their entire future and reality were being challenged
by competition from beyond the world? Who would be foolish
enough to cast humanity into conflict if they knew and understood
the greater challenge now facing the entire human family?

The Greater Community here has many beneficial aspects for you.
It is the one thing that can unite humanity and end its ceaseless
conflicts. It is the one thing that can force you to mature, to unite
and to cooperate for the protection of your world. It will force you to
be responsible where you are being irresponsible. It will force you to
be mature where you are being immature. It will force you to realize
that you must care for this world, that you must create a sustainable
existence here and that you cannot go into the universe to claim what
you have destroyed here in this world, for these resources are owned
by others, and you will have no power or efficacy to gain access to
them. And your freedom and your self-determination within this
larger arena of life will require that humanity be self-sufficient and
responsible for establishing its own solutions to difficult problems
here on Earth.

Humanity is still wild and reckless. Like an adolescent, it is beginning to feel its power, but it is not yet responsible. It is not yet mature enough to use this power effectively for its own benefit. It is not thinking of its future, and it does not realize the great risks it faces within this Greater Community. It does not yet have the self-confidence, the maturity or the skill to face this larger panorama of life.

This is your challenge. You cannot avoid it. There is nowhere to run and hide. Are you going to go hide in some other world? Are you going to pretend? Are you going to deny this reality? Are you going to think that this is irrelevant?

This is the great threshold that can uplift and unite humanity. It is also the great threshold that can undermine humanity. It has this power and this strength. It is your courage, your confidence and your self-determination now that will have to be brought to bear.

Technology is not your problem. Your problem has to do with courage, clarity and determination. You will not fail because of technology. You will fail because of the lack of wisdom, cooperation and awareness in your world. That is your great danger.

You have power. You have skills. You have wisdom. No one else can live in your world. It is biologically too complex for them. They need you. They need your cooperation. They need you to submit to them, willingly. They need to erode your self-confidence so that you feel you cannot resist them. They need you to deplete your resources so that you will become dependent upon them.

This is a fundamental education. Yet people have many ideas and beliefs that will blind them to the reality of their situation. Preference, denial, human conflict, humanity's degradation of the natural world—these all are putting you in a position of extreme powerlessness and vulnerability in the universe.

What would motivate you to change? It must be something very strong, very overbearing, something that you had not thought of before—a dilemma greater than anything you think you are facing today, a challenge from the universe that will awaken you to your vulnerability and to your set of circumstances.

This is the great threshold, and you must have the strength, the heart and the courage to face it and to realize you do not have an answer. You cannot figure this out yourself. You do not have all of the necessary information or the necessary perspective. That is why the Creator of all life is bringing this New Revelation into the world—to prepare humanity for the Great Waves of change and to prepare humanity for the realities of life in the Greater Community.

Humanity has a great destiny. Its destiny is to become a free and self-determined race in the universe. But in order to fulfill this destiny, you must become strong, united and determined. You must realize that your isolation in the universe is over, and that henceforth you will have to contend with those forces who seek to persuade you to become reliant upon them, who will seek to undermine your self-confidence, who will seek to establish their influence here in the world—in a world where they cannot live.

You will have many questions, and there are many things you must learn. The Revelation from God will answer many of these questions. But this will take [time] and require that you reconsider many things in the world today, that you see the world differently, that you view human conflict differently and that you recognize that your future and your destiny, your success and your failure, reside in the Greater

Community itself. If you can see this, it will be a great blessing. It will be a revelation. It will be a real turning point for you as an individual.

You will see that you must bring a greater sobriety and objectivity to bear and that the strength to do this lives within you—a deeper power, the power of Knowledge waiting to be discovered. This Knowledge must come forth in your life as an individual and must become stronger in the human family.

This is the requirement of freedom in the universe. This is the gift of facing a Greater Community of life. This is the gift of Revelation to you, who are now standing at the threshold of space.

CHAPTER 2

CONTACT WITH INTELLIGENT LIFE IN THE UNIVERSE

As revealed to
Marshall Vian Summers
on October 1, 2008
in Boulder, Colorado

The world is a beautiful place. It is a world of immense biological diversity. It is a world of tremendous wealth and value. The human family does not realize how significant a place this world really is in a universe of barren worlds.

You do not realize the significance and value this will be given by those races who are aware of your existence. Those few races who have been observing human behavior and human history, they—with only a few exceptions—view you as chaotic and barbaric. They are concerned that you are destroying the wealth of this world, a wealth that they want to have for themselves.

Humanity has evolved in a state of relative isolation, relative because the world has been visited throughout its history, particularly with the advent of humanity. Periodically, the world has been visited by different races coming to seek the biological wealth of the world and also to hide things of value in the world, things that the native peoples in earlier times would never find or suspect.

Your world has a long history of visitation, but colonization in the world by foreign races has never been successful, for reasons that you might not expect. Advanced technological races function mostly in sterile environments. To come into a world of such biological diversity, with countless biological agents, produces a hazard for such races. While they may be able to spend time in this world on board their own craft or even to build facilities here, the biological hazard of the world is too great, and the risk of contamination is too significant.

Humanity has adapted to these conditions with few exceptions, and so it is hard for you to imagine that an advanced race would have such difficulty being here. Even if they could breathe your atmosphere, which many races could not, they would have to face a great risk of contamination, for they do not have the adaptive abilities or the resistance to function in such a biologically diverse environment.

You, of course, have adapted to this with few exceptions. And some people think that with advanced technology you can overcome such obstacles. But biological contamination is a very serious problem within the context of visiting other worlds, particularly worlds where there is biological diversity that is foreign from your own native world. It is a problem of great significance in the universe amongst races who travel and engage in the complex array of involvements with other worlds.

The human family, of course, knows nothing of this, being that you are still isolated in the world and have not been able to escape the boundaries of your world in any significant way. It is still widely believed amongst the human family that the universe is a great empty place, and if there is intelligent life out there somewhere, it is very rare.

Because you have not yet passed through the threshold, a technological threshold that stands between you and traveling in this Greater Community of life in the universe, you cannot imagine how other races can travel from world to world. So you are handicapped both by your isolation and by your technological limitations.

But the truth of the matter is that beyond this solar system, you live in a greatly inhabited part of the universe. Beyond this solar system, there are great avenues of trade and many trading nations that have long established their networks of commerce. War and conflict have been suppressed, and freedom is rare within this larger arena of life.

Here is your world, a world of great value, a world of value to any technologically advanced race. For the vast majority of technologically advanced races have outstripped their own world's natural resources and must now travel and become engaged in complex and restrictive networks of trade to gain what they need— not only to provide for their technological requirements, but also for things that are more basic, such as biological materials for food production and the creation of medicine, and biological engineering and so forth.

It is hard to imagine for humanity how technological achievement has come at such a great price. Yet you are beginning to pay such a price within your own world at this time. As your technology begins to accelerate in its evolution and development, you find yourself outstripping your world's natural resources at a frightening pace. You find yourself degrading your natural environment and impacting even the climates of your own world.

Other races, of course, have followed this same destructive path only to find themselves greatly imperiled because they cannot provide for themselves, having damaged or disabled their own natural world's life-sustaining functions. Now they must seek resources beyond their world— resources that are owned by others, resources for which they will have to compromise themselves and accept the terms of engagement, which can be very restrictive.

Once these nations become part of these larger trading networks, they find that they must conform to the requirements and expectations of others or face the terrifying prospect of being denied the acquisition of resources.

War and conflict within such an environment become suppressed to maintain the stability and security of the trading networks. Should a nation resist or try to militarily seize what it needs, it will be opposed by hundreds of other worlds.

Humanity is still enthralled with the idea of growth and expansion. It has not matured to a place of realizing that stability and security represent its future stage of development. All races in the universe have had to face this reality, for you cannot keep expanding in the universe without facing unending conflict and instability.

In this respect, humanity is in a kind of adolescent stage. It is feeling its power and its possibilities. It is beginning to recognize it has greater potential. But it is irresponsible. It is mismanaging its world. It is focused on growth, and now it is hitting the limits of growth.

Never think that should you outstrip your world's resources, you can go into the universe to gain what you need. For the only way, living in such a highly populated part of the universe, that you would be able to do this would be to become a member, a very junior member in this case, of a larger trading network. This would be a great misfortune, for you would have to meet very restrictive terms of engagement. You would have to compromise yourself. And other nations would exert political influence over you, influence that you would find to be very repressive.

You would find yourself no longer preeminent within your own world, but now subjected to the influences and the requirements placed upon you by nations elsewhere—by nations that are not human and do not value what humanity values, nations that look upon your world and upon you as a resource to be exploited, to be used. Your lack of skill and sophistication within this larger environment would make you very, very vulnerable to exploitation and to manipulation.

That is why maintaining your self-sufficiency in this world is immensely important if humanity is to emerge into this Greater Community of intelligent life as a free and self-determined race. Here your conflicts must cease, and your management of the world's resources must be stabilized. Here your consumption of resources must be restricted, or you will have no future, you will lose your self-sufficiency and will have to meet whatever terms are placed before you by other nations, who now [would] seize a great opportunity to gain access to your world's wealth and strategic importance.

You are like the native people living in the heart of the jungle, in isolation. You have developed your culture there. You have developed your religious understanding there. You have developed your concept of God there. And you feel that your existence is so significant.

But when you encounter visitors from the outside, you will tend to misunderstand their presence and intentions—thinking they are here to help you, thinking they are here to benefit you, and you will be very susceptible to their offers of technology, to their inducements and to their seductions. You would be at risk of failing to see that they are merely resource explorers. Perhaps you would think of them as gods or advanced races of beings. And you could be mesmerized by their technology and fascinated by their abilities, all the while placing yourself in great danger of falling under their persuasions.

This reality and awareness is not fearful. It is just real. It is the reality of life. It is what intervention has taught you throughout history— that it is always carried out for self-interest, and those races who are being discovered face great danger of destruction and subjugation.

Humanity has great promise and a greater destiny in the universe. But in order for you to fulfill this promise and this destiny, you must meet three requirements. You must be self-sufficient. You must be united. And you must be extremely discreet. These are the three requirements for all free nations in the universe.

But at present, humanity is failing each one of these basic requirements. You are rapidly destroying your self-sufficiency by the mismanagement and overuse of your world's resources.

You are hardly united and still value your conflicts and your distinctions from one another to such a great degree that human unity on a large scale has not yet been established, even in facing critical problems in the world itself.

And you are hardly discreet, broadcasting all of your strengths and weaknesses out into the universe for any discreet observer to see. No advanced technological society broadcasts in this way. That is why you will not find radio signals coming from space because no one who values their security ever broadcasts in such a manner.

Humanity does not realize what will be required for it to build and maintain its freedom and sovereignty in this world. It is a very critical problem that very few people are aware of.

That is why humanity is still in an adolescent phase. It is reckless. It is irresponsible. It does not see itself in relationship to a larger arena of life. It is self-preoccupied. It is self-centered. It does not see what will be required of it to function within a Greater Community of life—a Greater Community that is not filled with human beings, a Greater Community where all races are searching for resources.

You might hope that other races have gained a kind of magical self-sufficiency where they do not need to gain resources from other worlds. But in reality, this is not the case. Greater technology requires a greater dependence on resources. If any nation has outstripped its own world of its natural inheritance and has lost its self-sufficiency as a result, then it is forced to engage with other races, and it is forced to accommodate to the requirements that such networks of trade require.

Here you would find it to be very difficult to maintain whatever degree of freedom you have established thus far in the world. For free races do not coexist well with races that are not free, with governments that do not value individual freedom. There would be great pressure from the outside for you not only to restrict this freedom, but to eliminate it altogether.

Therefore, do not think of the universe as a kind of wilderness waiting to be explored and exploited. This part of your galaxy is highly inhabited, and there is no wilderness here.

This gives you advantages and disadvantages. The advantage is that war and conflict are suppressed in this part of the galaxy. It is not like your movies or your concepts. There are no huge empires here that govern everyone, for large empires are difficult to maintain and rarely survive for long in the Greater Community.

That means that no one can take your world by force, for conquest by force is not allowed. It is suppressed to maintain stability and security in this region of space. Conquest by force is suppressed. It will not happen here.

Nations will seek to gain advantage in your world through other means, through the powers of persuasion—by amplifying your needs and your inability to fulfill those needs, by persuading you that only they can guide you and lead you and provide for you what you really need.

Humanity will not be overcome by the use of force. It will be overcome, if it is overcome, by the power of inducement and persuasion. This, of course, you must resist. To resist this, you must recognize the three requirements to remain free and sovereign within this world.

For humanity's isolation is now over. You are destroying the natural environment. This has generated intervention from other races who are now functioning in your world, seeking to establish themselves here, seeking to gain advantage and dominance within the world without the use of force.

To those few people who are aware of their presence, they will present themselves as beneficial and benign, proclaiming that they have no war and that they live in peace. And through the demonstration of their technology, they will try to impress you that they, more than you, understand what will bring stability and security to your world.

But it is all a deception, for they are here to plant themselves. Regardless of their wonderful proclamations and their great promises to a struggling humanity, they are here to plant themselves. As it has happened so often in your own history, the native peoples are easily persuaded and do not recognize the real threat of the interventions that they face.

CONTACT WITH INTELLIGENT LIFE
IN THE UNIVERSE

In the universe, humanity has really two different kinds of encounters with life beyond its borders. You will have potential allies, and you will have competitors. You do not yet have enemies because you are not trying to exert your force beyond this solar system.

So you do not have enemies, but you do have many competitors. Restrained from using force, they will use other means to gain access to this world. They will come here in small groups, establishing networks, establishing liaisons with certain selected leaders in positions of power in government, commerce and religion. They will attempt to establish different influences within your religious communities and religious understanding. They will seek to establish a physical presence in the world even though they cannot breathe your atmosphere and cannot face the biological hazards of trying to exist here outside their own protective enclosures.

They are not here to destroy you, but to use you, for they cannot live in this world. So they need you to work for them. And they will promise you anything. And they will assure you that you yourselves cannot solve your problems, in order to gain this power of influence over you.

This is how a small group of resource explorers could overtake the entire human family without the use of force. They will prey upon your conflicts and your inability to resolve these conflicts, emphasizing that they, more than you, have the power and the capability to meet the growing needs of humanity.

This, of course, will persuade and induce many people as humanity loses confidence in itself, in its leaders and in its institutions. This will create a vacuum of confidence, which can easily be filled by the Intervention that exists in the world today.

So you have competitors, and you have potential allies. Your Allies will send you their wisdom as they have already done in a series of Briefings, Briefings from the Allies of Humanity. But they will not interfere. They are not present in your world.

All those visiting your world at this time are part of the Intervention. And there is more than one group. Within each group, there are different races of beings functioning at different levels of responsibility. So the Intervention has many faces, and this will be very confusing to you here on the ground.

Your Allies will not interfere because they realize that if they interfere, they will have to manipulate your perception and your understanding. In order for you even to act correctly, they would have to manipulate you. They would have to control you. This they will not do because they are freedom-loving races. They know, through the lessons of life in the universe, that the attempt to control the future and destiny of another world will require subjugation. And this they will not do.

Free races in your local universe are rare, and they must remain discreet. If they attempt to control or manipulate the fate of a world such as yours, then their discretion will be broken. So they must support you without intervention.

You do not yet have the maturity or the wisdom about life in the universe to see the importance of this. Yet even in your own experience at this time, you see when one nation tries to control the behavior or perception of another nation, it leads to conquest and domination, great conflict and the destruction of those people and those nations that are being controlled. You see this within your own experience.

CONTACT WITH INTELLIGENT LIFE
IN THE UNIVERSE

Life does not change when you enter the Greater Community. The lessons of life are still the same. They are only being played out on a much larger scale with many different races. The level of complexity increases, but the reality is the same.

Those races who are the potential allies of humanity realize that humanity is not yet ready for contact. The human family does not have the unity, the maturity, the discretion or the strength yet to engage in the very challenging situations and involvements of intelligent life in the universe.

You are naïve. You are unprepared and not adapted to this demanding environment. You do not realize the risks. You are ambitious. You are idealistic. You are self-centered. You think the universe revolves around you and that anyone who would visit your world would be here to bring you gifts and to assist you.

This is so very naïve, but it is understandable because this is how races living in isolation perceive themselves. This is how they view the prospects of engaging with life beyond their borders.

There is so much here for humanity to learn about life in the universe. There is so much wisdom you must gain. There is so much caution you must exercise. There are so many important distinctions that you must make.

You are unprepared. And you cannot prepare yourself because you do not know what you are preparing for, or what it will require or what the risks really are.

God knows what humanity is facing in the Greater Community. God knows that humanity cannot prepare itself for the realities of life in the universe. That is why a New Message has been sent into the world:

to prepare humanity for the great environmental and economic problems that the world is facing here and to prepare humanity for its encounters with intelligent life in the universe.

Only God knows what is happening in the universe, without deception and distortion. Only God knows what is coming over the horizon of life for humanity. Only God really knows what humanity must see and know and do to build human unity, to regain and sustain your self-sufficiency in this world and to build the necessary discretion and discernment you will need to function successfully in this larger arena of life.

For you are destined for the Greater Community. But first you must survive the Greater Community. And you must mature and become wise regarding your engagement with other races.

No one should be intervening in your world at this time. This represents unethical behavior. It is being carried out for self-interest. It is deceptive. It is dangerous.

Humanity is not yet ready for contact, but contact is happening. And the rules of engagement are not being established by you, as they should be, but by others, who are functioning here in secret, concealing their intentions and their activities from the human family.

Never think that no one can reach your shores. Do not think the universe is limited by the accomplishments of human science. Do not think that your understanding of the universe is complete.

You are a young race. There are much older races. There are much older civilizations. Life has been evolving in the universe for a very long time. Even before humanity existed in this world, space travel was established and was carried out in countless regions by countless races. You are the new kid on the block, a youngster, freshly emerging from your long tribal history.

Civilization is recent in this world, but there are many older civilizations, even in your region of space. They have attained stability, stability humanity has not yet acquired. But stability is either established through suppression and control or through the very careful and difficult process of nurturing individual and collective freedom. Most races have chosen the former path, for it is far more expedient.

Freedom is difficult. It tends to be disorderly. It does not have the kind of stability that other races have acquired through dominance and control. But freedom is more important. It is more significant. It is more creative. And it is more beneficial. That is why the preservation of human freedom in the face of the Greater Community is so extremely important.

The human family is obsessed with its own dilemmas and its own corruption, its own problems and its own failures. But you do not see that your greatest challenge is being placed before you by the Intervention that is occurring in your world today, by those races who seek to take advantage of a weak and divided humanity. And you do not yet see that your destruction of your natural inheritance will prevent you in the future from maintaining your autonomy, your freedom and your self-determination within this world.

The three requirements for freedom in the universe are three requirements you cannot change. They are what every race who has been able to build and maintain individual and collective freedom has had to accommodate. The challenges of these three requirements cannot be escaped. But humanity is as yet unaware of what is required of it to function within this larger arena of life.

Do not think that races will come here out of curiosity. Do not think that races will come to bring humanity gifts because they are so enraptured with your culture or your possibilities. In the universe around you, visitation to other worlds is actually quite rare and is only carried out for self-interest.

While there are other races who might want to know you or are curious about you, they will not expend the energy or commit the resources to establishing themselves here for altruistic purposes. They will come because they need what the world has. And whatever they might offer you, they will want many things in return.

This is the reality of life in the universe. Everyone is struggling to gain access to resources. Everyone is facing competition in life.

Those races who have been able to remain free are very discreet. They do not involve themselves in networks of trade. They do not establish relationships with worlds that are not free. They are discreet. They are hidden. They maintain connections with one another through various means.

This is the price of freedom in a universe where freedom is rare. You can see this within your own world. It is not a mystery. A free nation in your world will have difficulty dealing with other nations where freedom is suppressed or denied its citizens. Whatever alliances you create here will be uneasy and difficult to maintain.

How much greater will this difficulty be between races who are entirely different from each other, who have different values, different cultures, different histories. The problems that exist nation to nation in your world are far greater when dealing with other races of beings whose language, culture and values are entirely different from one another.

God has sent a New Revelation into the world to reveal the realities of life in the universe and the things that humanity must see, know and do to prepare for this.

God's New Message also reveals the Great Waves of change that are coming to your world that are largely the result of humanity's misuse and mismanagement of the world. Resource depletion, environmental degradation, violent weather, increasing political and economic instability and the risk of war and competition over the remaining resources—these are the Great Waves of change that are converging within your world.

The Intervention that is being carried out here is aware of these great changes and will attempt to use them for its own benefit. Humanity has only to be persuaded that a foreign race has greater power and greater abilities to give over the keys to this world, to acquiesce, to submit and to allow an Intervention to establish itself here.

This has happened before in your own history, where native races allowed foreign intervention to occur only to find themselves displaced, overwhelmed and even destroyed. Life has taught you this. Life has taught you the lessons of intervention.

But many people today still want things from the visitors. Having lost faith in humanity, they now look to other forces to give them encouragement and direction.

The true Allies of Humanity are not intervening in the world because intervention leads to subjugation. They are not giving humanity technology because they know that this technology would only be turned into weaponry and used by selfish and exploitive forces in the world. They are not seducing you with their power. They are not tantalizing you with their technology. For they know that humanity must grow and become far wiser than it is today in order to have a chance to maintain its freedom and self-sufficiency in the universe.

Your isolation is over. Intervention is occurring in your world and has been here for some time. But humanity is not seeing it. It is not recognizing it. Even amongst those few people who are aware of the foreign presence here, they are not interpreting this correctly for the most part. They think it is a blessing. Or perhaps they think there are good visitors and bad visitors because they still want something from the visitation.

Whenever you want something from encountering another, you place yourself in jeopardy. You lose your objectivity. You become open to persuasion and manipulation.

Humanity has the power and the wealth. It can maintain its freedom in the universe, but it must function very differently than it is functioning today to meet the three requirements that are placed before it to be a free and self-determined race.

Contact has begun, but it is not what you think. It is greatly misunderstood and denied in the world. It is the greatest event in human history, and humanity is not prepared. And for this reason, God has sent a New Message into the world to prepare humanity for the Greater Community and to warn and prepare humanity for the Great Waves of change that are coming to the world and that are already striking the shores of the world, influencing the lives of millions of people.

CONTACT WITH INTELLIGENT LIFE
IN THE UNIVERSE

This represents a far greater education for humanity and a Revelation unlike any of God's former Revelations to the human family. For you are entering a new arena of life. You are passing through a great and profound threshold in your evolution.

Humanity's religions cannot prepare it for the future, and that is why a New Revelation is being sent here now. It comes from the Creator of all life. It emphasizes human freedom; human sovereignty in this world; human unity and cooperation to meet the challenges of life here; and Wisdom from the Greater Community that humanity must acquire if it is to function successfully within this larger arena of intelligent life. It is a great gift of love to a struggling humanity. But it is very challenging. It is very demanding. And it is very reassuring.

God has given humanity a deeper Knowledge that resides within each person, a deeper intelligence beyond the realm and the reach of the intellect—an intelligence that cannot be corrupted, persuaded or adulterated in any way. It is this power of Knowledge that represents your core strength and the source of your integrity and your ability to see beyond deception in any form.

Humanity is still valued by free races in your local universe because the potential for Self-Knowledge still exists here. It has not been eradicated. It has not been lost, as it has been lost by so many other races and nations.

That is why the New Message from God emphasizes The Way of Knowledge and the power of Knowledge in the individual, for this is the source of your freedom. And it is this, more than anything else, that will enable you to see, to know and to have the strength to act on your own behalf in the face of other intervening forces.

It is God's greatest gift to you as an individual and to the human family. And it will be your gift to other races in the universe. But first you must establish yourself as a free and self-determined people. You must learn Wisdom from the Greater Community. You must establish your own rules of engagement regarding any visitation to your world. And you must exercise your authority in this way to gain the recognition and the respect of other nations in this region of space.

It is a great challenge, but it is one that will unite you, redeem you and give you courage and strength—things that are now fading in the world, that are being lost. Humanity must regain its confidence. It must regain the power and the presence of Knowledge. It must unite for its own survival and well-being. And it must cultivate individual freedom here and face the challenge of living within the environmental constraints of this world.

If you can do this, you have a greater future in the universe. And it is this future now that represents your greatest challenge. For the future is here now. The Greater Community is here now.

Long before you are able to go out into space in any significant way, contact will occur and is occurring even now. And it is for this that you must prepare.

CHAPTER 3

FACING THE GREATER COMMUNITY

As revealed to
Marshall Vian Summers
on April 22, 2010
in Boulder, Colorado

For centuries, the Earth has been visited periodically by races seeking biological resources. For the most part, they had very little interaction with the native peoples, often focusing on parts of the world where there was very little human habitation.

Over the millennia, there have been several attempts to establish permanent settlements here, but the biological hazard of the world was too great for races living in sterile environments. These missions failed and had to be withdrawn.

The record of visitations can be found in many ancient scriptures, but humanity still does not understand that it lives in a very well-inhabited part of the universe, a part of the universe where there are old races, very well-established networks of trade and commerce, a region of space where war has been suppressed and where there are very few really free nations.

So humanity, in all of its claimed brilliance and creativity, remains profoundly ignorant about the conditions of life beyond this world, the nature of interactions in this part of the universe and what all that really means for a struggling humanity.

The last century a new kind of visitor came to the world, unlike those who came before, visitors seeking to establish themselves in the world as humanity gained greater global predominance and was able to establish global networks of trade and commerce, communications and so forth.

This new visitor was not just here looking for biological samples or exploring rich and diverse biological regions of the world. They were here to scheme how to position themselves as the providers for humanity, particularly as human civilization began to outstrip the world's natural resources and energy resources.

Their presence is small, and yet they have been witnessed all over the world. They seek to operate in a surreptitious manner and do not reveal their intentions or their activities.

This, then, is an Intervention into the world. It is not a visitation. It is not occurring as a result of humanity's request or the request of any person, nation or government. It is an Intervention with a plan, carried out not by military forces, but by small networks of resource explorers and economic collectives—a lower order, ethically speaking, of civilized life in the universe—here to search not only for resources but for influence in the world, in worlds such as yours, which are so very rare.

Humanity, then, is facing competition from beyond the world—a clever and cunning competition, a competition that does not rely upon weapons, a competition that does not rely upon conquest—not outright conquest, but instead a devious planting of influence at this time as humanity begins to exhaust the world's natural resources and is facing a growing crisis in food, the availability of energy, and even water in many places.

[It is] a time where humanity will be facing the Great Waves of change, brought on by humanity's misuse and abuse of the world and overuse and overexploitation of its vital resources. This is an opportune time for an Intervention to take place, and while the world has been watched for a very long time, now is the opportunity to establish a new kind of influence over the human family.

If humanity knew anything about life in the universe, you would resist any visitation to the world. You would not be foolish and idealistic regarding this. Your governments would prepare your peoples. Everyone would be watchful, watching the skies, reporting any sightings.

But, alas, this is not the case, and humanity remains ignorant and vulnerable to the powers of persuasion that exist in this part of the universe. While outright conquest of a world such as yours is not permitted by the networks of trade, there are other means for gaining influence and access to emerging worlds such as your own.

These forces, then, are not evil. They are not satanic. They are merely aggressive and exploitive. All races in the universe need resources, and those technologically advanced races that have outstripped their world's resources must now trade, barter and search for the things that they need and for the things that they can sell and trade and so forth.

It is a complicated environment. It is a very competitive environment. One must be skillful and alert. And that is why the free nations and races in this part of the galaxy must exercise great discretion. They must have great unity within their own worlds. And they must be as self-sufficient as possible because once you become engaged in large networks of trade, they will control the terms of engagement, and they will influence all who are a part of them.

For free worlds do not co-exist well with those that are not free. Free peoples do not easily engage with those who are not free. You can see this even within your own world today.

Humanity's destiny is in the universe, but whether the human family will be free and sovereign or whether it will be a client of other powers, dominated by other powers, controlled economically and politically by other powers, remains to be seen.

Your world is rich. It is rich biologically. These resources are extremely valuable in a universe of barren worlds—worlds that have been stripped bare by aggressive races, worlds that have been exploited and colonized by other races. You know not of the wealth of this world.

People still believe so foolishly that the universe is just a big, empty place awaiting their exploitation and exploration. But once you leave this solar system, you begin to enter territory that is controlled by others, and you have not the power nor the skill to compete with them.

God knows that you are entering the Greater Community of life in the universe and that humanity is vulnerable, ignorant and superstitious. It is dominated by the belief that it is important in the universe.

Recognizing this great peril, the Creator of all life has sent the New Message into the world to prepare humanity to face the Great Waves of change that are coming to the world and to prepare humanity for its future and destiny within a Greater Community of life in the universe.

This preparation must come from God because you cannot prepare yourselves. You do not have the time. You do not have the wisdom. And you are facing Intervention in the world that is growing in strength with each passing year. How could you possibly prepare yourself for an environment that you know nothing about?

Another race in the universe could not really prepare you for life in the Greater Community fully because no other race in the universe fully understands humanity's history, humanity's temperament, humanity's strengths and weaknesses. Though humanity has been studied by the Intervention, it knows not of these deeper matters.

You have allies in the universe—the Allies of Humanity. But they do not know a great deal about you. They only want to see you have a chance at emerging into this larger arena of life as a free and sovereign people, for they support freedom in the universe. They do not want to see humanity, with all of its talents and accomplishments, overtaken through the cunning and guile of those who are here in the world today to take advantage of a weak and vulnerable humanity.

There are no neutral parties in this matter. Humanity has a few Allies and many competitors. But it is important for you to understand that your Allies will not come here to defend the world, for they too must live with great discretion. And they realize, because they are intelligent and wise, that they cannot control the world, and if they attempted to do so, it would only lead to domination. That is why no free race is in the world today interfering in human affairs.

The Intervention is cunning. It will promise you peace and equanimity. It will promise you free energy and great wealth if only you will follow them. But these are things they cannot deliver, for they do not have these things. They are here searching because they have great needs. They will not destroy the human family but only seek to engage it and make you compliant and dependent upon them.

It is a situation of the gravest importance in the world and the gravest challenge and threat to human freedom—greater than any challenge you can imagine today. Only the destruction of the world's life-sustaining environment, which is represented by the Great Waves of change, can compete with this for importance.

Humanity must learn about the realities of life in the universe. It must learn about the spirituality of life in the universe. It must learn to expand its religious understanding to encompass a God of the universe, not simply a God of the world or a God of a race or a God of one place alone.

Humanity must learn how to discern friend from foe and how to strengthen your own self-sufficiency as a guarantee of your future freedom—freedom from intervention, freedom from manipulation, freedom from seduction. You must gain a greater cooperation between nations. This will only really be possible facing the Great Waves of change and facing competition from the universe.

These two great threats, either of which could destroy human civilization, have the power then to engage nations and peoples, governments and leaders, to recognize the great peril facing the human family and to gain a greater cooperation to protect the world, to establish your boundaries to space and to establish your own terms of engagement regarding who can visit this world and under what conditions that is permissible.

But this is not the case, and humanity is far from establishing this level of cooperation amongst its nations and peoples. Divided, you are easily manipulated. United, you can withstand the pressures that are now being placed upon the human family.

The tragedy of the Intervention is that every year thousands of people are taken for experimentation, for mind control, and many are not returned. And those that are returned are never quite the same because they are being controlled. They are being used. Some are being used to support the Intervention, to speak for the Intervention. And some are simply being used as a biological resource.

The complexity of this is revealed in God's New Revelation. The meaning of this is revealed in God's New Revelation. Yet do not think that this is in any way beneficial to any individual in the world, or to the human family as a whole.

Therefore, the Creator of all life must alert and educate the human family regarding a reality of which it is profoundly unaware and in many cases profoundly mistaken in its assumptions and beliefs.

You must think of yourselves as the native peoples of the world now and know that any other race that seeks to make a claim to this place, for any reason, represents a competitive power in the universe.

For humanity has established networks of trade and communications that other races can use. You have built an infrastructure that other races will seek to use for themselves. And that is why intervention did not happen at an earlier time.

It is part of the misfortune of becoming powerful. You gain a greater recognition here. You become valuable to others. You become useful to others, whereas before humanity was far too primitive for any kind of meaningful engagement or exploitation.

This is a very difficult message to hear, and it requires serious consideration to understand. It is a reality for which you need great assistance because you do not know what exists beyond your borders. People's understanding of life in the universe is conditioned by movies and fantasies and fantastic tales that have nothing to do with the reality itself.

There are many people in the world today who have a Greater Community connection, who can respond to these things. Somehow at a deeper level, they know they are a part of preparing for the Greater Community. They have come into the world with this understanding, given to them by God before they came, planted deeply in their deeper Knowledge—a Knowledge that would not arise until much later in life, until they were mature enough and stable enough to begin to consider greater things.

There is only one preparation for the Greater Community in the world today, and that is part of God's New Revelation. No foreign race could give this to you, for no foreign race fully understands the deeper spiritual nature of humanity.

Even your Allies abroad will only seek to alert you to the presence of the Intervention and to teach you some vital and important things about life in the universe around you. But they cannot prepare you for the Greater Community. They are only playing a very small part in this.

It takes great courage to face these things, great sobriety. But if you consider that competition is part of nature, and if you consider the meaning of intervention in humanity's own history, you will see that intervention is always carried out for self-interest and, in almost all cases, has a devastating impact upon the native peoples, wherever it has occurred in the past.

You cannot be foolish here. You cannot be idealistic. You cannot think that everyone in the universe is here to bless and support the human family: a small, hidden race in the universe, unknown except to a very few of your neighbors and other forces in this part of the galaxy.

Do not be foolish in thinking that the Intervention is here to benefit humanity in any way. That would be a fatal error. It is an error that your ancestors have made—the native peoples of this world—in encountering foreign intervention for the first time.

No, you must resist the Intervention. And you must prepare for the Greater Community. In this regard, the human family as a whole must begin to grow up and must outgrow its tribal conflicts, its bitter disputes, its historical animosities amongst nations and tribes and groups.

You have a greater competition to face in the universe. You have a greater set of problems to deal with. How are you going to prepare the human family for the Great Waves of change? How are you going to provide for the peoples of the world in an environment of declining resources?

It is a time of reckoning for humanity, a great evolutionary threshold that all races must face eventually. Here you have two choices. If humanity is to be free and sovereign in this world and protect itself from intervention and manipulation, it must meet the three requirements that all free races must establish, [or not].

You must be united sufficiently to overcome war and conflict within your own world. You must be self-sufficient, which means you do not need foreign resources or alien technologies. And you must be extremely discreet, which means you are not broadcasting all of your foolishness and weakness out into space for everyone to see.

You have a natural right to this solar system, but do not seek to go beyond or you will become engaged in the Greater Community, and it is far more powerful than you will ever be. It has strengths humanity has not cultivated. It has technology humanity does not possess. It has a long-term understanding of the engagement with other races so unlike one another that humanity does not yet possess.

God knows you could not prepare for the Greater Community in time, and that is why part of God's New Revelation is dedicated to this preparation. The Creator of all life has called humanity's Allies in this region of space to send their wisdom here in a series of Briefings, Briefings from the Allies of Humanity.

Your Allies will not interfere. They will not come to control or manipulate human understanding. They are only sharing their wisdom and alerting you to the presence of the Intervention, and what that really means for you now, and how it can be offset.

If the governments of the world understood humanity's great vulnerability, war would end tomorrow. There would be a great discussion on how to protect the world, how to defend the world and how to sustain the world's resources so that humanity will not fall prey to foreign intervention and persuasion.

For should you deplete the resources of this world, others will come to provide them, and you will have no choice but to agree to their terms and their requirements. That would be the end of humanity's freedom and progress in the universe—a tragic ending to a very promising race.

The Intervention will seek to make you lose faith in your leaders, in your institutions and even within yourself, leading you to believe that only they can provide for you and guide you truly. This persuasion is already being cast over many people.

The Intervention will seek to stimulate and exacerbate conflicts within the world to weaken the strongest powers, to lead them into engagements that are fruitless and destructive. This is already happening in the world.

But humanity has time, and it has hope. You can offset the Intervention. You can prepare for the Great Waves of change. And you must prepare for the realities of life in the universe, which you are now encountering increasingly with each passing year.

The gift has been given. The preparation is here. God's Revelation has been given and is being protected by the Messenger, who has been sent into the world to receive God's New Message for humanity.

Come to learn of these things, and you will see with your own eyes, and you will know with your heart what is true. There is no deception here. But you must know this for yourself. You do not yet know friend from foe. You do not know a gift from a danger. You do not know the meaning of providence, nor can you distinguish that from manipulation yet. But your heart will know because you have a deeper Knowledge within you that can clearly see the difference between these things.

It is time to prepare for the Greater Community of life. It is time to learn of the Intervention in the world. It is time to prepare for the Great Waves of change that will affect all the peoples and nations. There is so much to be done, and time is of the essence. You do not have a great deal of time, and you certainly do not have time to waste in these matters.

The Creator of all life has sent a warning into the world, but also has sent a blessing and a preparation to prepare humanity for that which it cannot yet see, to strengthen the human family, to reveal the meaning of your spirituality at the level of a deeper Knowledge, to sow the seeds of cooperation and harmony, duty and responsibility so that the human family may have a future, so the human family may be [self-sufficient] and stable and secure in a universe full of intelligent life.

For this is not a human universe you are facing. It is very different. You know not of its requirements, its dangers and its opportunities. These must be revealed to you through the Grace and the Power of God, for this is the only truly trustworthy Source. And this is the Source that knows beyond deception, beyond self-interest, beyond corruption and beyond misunderstanding.

Freedom is rare in the universe. The wise are far and few between in the universe, for most choose the path of technological power and advancement and lose their native abilities and the power of Knowledge within themselves, only to become dominated, only to become encased in a seemingly permanent manner, in dreadful technological societies where the individual is but a unit, a component, where individual freedom is very rare, where the deeper talents of the individual are either ignored entirely or are used to support the interests of the state.

Freedom is precious. Do not assume that it will be yours. You must always care for it, protect it and defend it if necessary. This is the price of freedom in the universe because the physical universe is where the separated have come to live, and the power and the grace that the Creator has given to each individual is largely unknown here.

There is so much for you to learn and to unlearn regarding this because it is the greatest education you could ever have, and you cannot learn it in your colleges or universities. Your experts know not of it. It is new Knowledge for a new world. And it will be the most important Knowledge for your future, your freedom and your destiny.

CHAPTER 4

ENTERING THE GREATER COMMUNITY

As revealed to
Marshall Vian Summers
on May 27, 2011
in Boulder, Colorado

God's New Revelation opens the doors to a universe of intelligent life, providing perspective, insight and understanding never available before.

The human family does not realize its vulnerability to this Greater Community nor its relationship with this Greater Community.

Living in isolation for so very long, your whole notion of yourself, your notion of Creation and the Divine, are very much associated with this one world alone. And yet so many people in the world today have roots in the Greater Community, for much of their previous experience [occurred] there before coming into this world, in this life.

It is like you are an isolated tribe never discovered by the outer world, not knowing the greater powers that exist around you and completely unprepared for the day that your existence would be discovered from the outside.

But of course, humanity has been broadcasting out into space, quite foolishly of course, and so your presence is well known to your neighbors and to other groups who are watching the world with great interest.

For some, you have been studied for a very long time. While they might find your deeper nature incomprehensible, your outer behavior can be easily discerned and is quite predictable.

You are standing at the threshold of an entirely different reality, a non-human universe—a universe where human values and aspirations are not universally shared, a universe where your existence and where your importance are of little or no consequence, except to those races who either seek to support human freedom in the world or those races who seek to take it from you.

The Greater Community will alter how you see yourself, how nations here interact with one another and the whole priority of humanity. Its impact can be extremely beneficial if you can understand it correctly.

For it is the Greater Community that will finally persuade your nations to cooperate, to unite for the preservation of the world and the protection of the human family.

It is the Greater Community that will show you that you cannot afford your ceaseless conflicts here on Earth, that your resources here are precious and your self-sufficiency is of the greatest importance.

With this awareness, you would not continue to squander the world at the terrible pace that you are doing so now. You would not foolishly think the universe is there for the taking once you exhaust the wealth of this world. You would understand that this world is all that you have.

This world, this solar system, is all that you have. Beyond this, you are entering regions owned or controlled by others, and you cannot take this from them.

ENTERING THE GREATER COMMUNITY

You do not know the rules of engagement in the universe or the relations between nations or what is allowed and what is not allowed in this Greater Community of life. You are like the child entering the metropolis—innocent, assuming, unaware.

People want many things from visitors here. They expect many things. People feel they are very important in the universe and that others would naturally come here to help you and to give you what you wanted and needed. People think contact is kind of a thrilling adventure, a holiday from the mundanity of human life. They want to think that this contact would be very positive and beneficial because they do not have the strength, the courage or the preparation to consider it in any other way.

God's Revelation is providing you a window into this Greater Community of life, a window that only God could provide. For there is nothing in the universe that God is not aware of.

No race can certainly make such a claim. No race has the comprehension of even this one galaxy. No race has a comprehension of the deeper nature of humanity. Even those few races in this region of space who are free and self-determined, even they cannot fully understand what human nature really means.

But everyone in the universe is seeking resources, and the more technologically advanced nations are very dependent upon this. You do not reach a place where this need ceases to exist because as you advance technologically, the need escalates in response to it.

Humanity does not know it is at a great threshold, a great turning point, a turning point that will create a future unlike the past. Living in a declining world, a world of declining resources and shrinking opportunities, you do not see your great vulnerability to space.

Your borders are unguarded. Your people are unaware. Your governments are subsumed in their internal difficulties and problems with one another.

This world, such a beautiful place, so rich biologically, with so many important resources that are difficult to find in a universe of barren worlds.

The Revelation from God must awaken you to the realities, the difficulties and the opportunities of emerging into a Greater Community of life. None of God's previous Revelations were required to do this because the need was not there. Humanity had not progressed that far.

But you now have a global civilization—diffracted, conflicted, destructive, heedless and irresponsible, but it is a world community nonetheless. You have global communication. You have a global commerce, and for many people, a growing global awareness. It is at this point that intervention will be attempted. It is at this point that humanity becomes a prize to be claimed.

For those who will come here and who are here already cannot live in the biologically complex world that you inhabit and to which you are adapted. They need human assistance. They need human allegiance. They need human participation in order to gain sovereignty and control here. And they will take advantage of your expectations, your desires, your fantasies and your grievances to establish this position for themselves.

Look at the history of intervention in your world. Look how easily native peoples succumbed to the presence of foreign intervention. This must not be your fate.

If you begin to think within this larger arena of life, you will begin to see things you could not see before, and you will see that human unity and cooperation are not simply a desirable future goal or a preferred option, but instead a necessity to assure the freedom and the future of the human family.

The Intervention seeks not to destroy you, but to use you, to use you for their own purposes. This is a reality you cannot escape, and the deception that will be cast upon the human family and the pacification that it will cast upon the human family to submit, to acquiesce, are very strong and compelling.

Having lost faith in human leadership and institutions, people will look to other powers in the universe to guide them, believing fervently that a beneficial force will come here to restore and to save humanity from itself. It is this expectation, this desire, however unconscious it might be, that the Intervention will utilize for its own purposes.

Your freedom is precious, to whatever extent it has been established in the world. It has been gained through great effort and human sacrifice. It must be protected with great vigilance.

You are concerned only with each other in this regard. But now you have greater concerns, and with those concerns, a greater need to become educated about life in the universe and prepared for the meaning of this difficult and hazardous engagement.

Those who are allied to humanity, the free races, they will not intervene here, for intervention to them is [a] violation. They realize that even if they could gain your confidence and trust, they would have to maintain a controlling presence here in order to guide you into the Greater Community. This, they cannot do. They realize that humanity will have to struggle and suffer even to come to a point of recognition and responsibility regarding its future and destiny here.

They can only advise. They will send their Briefings, the Briefings from the Allies of Humanity. This they have done as part of God's New Revelation, for the Creator knows that you must realize that you are not totally alone in the universe and that freedom and self-determination exist and have been achieved by others. But this is not an easy achievement, and it has basic requirements.

People are shocked by these things, not because they are untrue or even that they seem sensational, but because they have never been thinking about it, and they do not even really want to think about it, it is so big and complex and challenging.

But this is your world. This is why you have come. You did not come to sleep on a beautiful planet, but to help preserve it and protect the human family from decline and from subjugation.

Human conflict is wasting you away. Ignorant, foolish and unaware of what exists at your borders, human conflict is wasting you away.

It is time for humanity to mature, to grow up, to realize you are living in a Greater Community of life—a Greater Community you cannot control, a Greater Community that is beyond your efforts, your technology and even your comprehension.

That is why the Creator of all life is bringing the Revelation about the Greater Community into the world. It is time now—as humanity stands at the brink of a declining world, a world of declining resources and growing economic and political upheaval and instability; a time when the religions of the world have become partisans in an ongoing conflict and competition for human acceptance and leadership; a time when the poorer nations are running out of resources and the rich nations are falling into great indebtedness.

It is the perfect time for intervention. It is the necessary time for a greater human awareness to emerge and with it a greater responsibility to the world—not just to one's nation or one's group or one's religious affiliation, but to all of humanity. For if nations fail, the whole world could fail. If intervention is successful in one part of the world, it threatens the future of everyone here.

People are full of grievance. They are full of needs. They are full of, in some cases, desperate needs—poverty and oppression. The leaders of the world are either blind or cannot communicate what they have been told, what they see and know. So the peoples of the nations remain ignorant about the greatest event in human history, the greatest challenge to human freedom and sovereignty and the greatest opportunity for human unity and cooperation.

For you will not be able to engage with a Greater Community of life as a warring and conflicted set of tribes and nations. You will have no strength and efficacy there, and your vulnerability will be so apparent to others.

Humanity is destroying the wealth of the world, and that too has prompted intervention.

There is so much for you to learn. It cannot be communicated in a few words, but in a great series of teachings, which are part of God's Revelation.

Here a Christian must become a Christian with a Greater Community awareness. A Muslim becomes a Muslim with a Greater Community awareness. A Buddhist and a Jew gain a greater panorama of life to which their religious teachings must become relevant. If religion in the world is to educate and to enlighten, it must have this greater capacity and awareness.

You cannot be fooling around in the face of the Greater Community or in the face of the Great Waves of change that are already occurring in the world. It is time to grow up.

Humanity has great strengths. You have not lost your connection to the deeper Knowledge that exists within each person. You have not become a regimented, secular, technological society, which are so common in the universe. You have not lost your freedom or your greater sensibilities entirely, though that is being threatened with each passing day.

The needs of life are fundamental everywhere. Advanced technology does not relieve you of these needs entirely and in fact can escalate them tremendously. Do you think that great technological societies in the universe are not desperate for resources, resources that they now cannot create themselves but must trade for and negotiate for, from far, far away? They have lost their self-determination. They are controlled now by the very networks of trade upon which they depend.

To be free in the universe you must be self-sufficient, you must be united, and you must be very discreet. Those are the requirements that every nation, every world, every race must establish in a Greater Community of life.

Here you can see the danger and the seduction of humanity receiving technology and resources from beyond the world. What a great attraction that would be. What a great seduction that is.

Once you lose your self-sufficiency, everything is lost that you value. For you will not be able to establish the terms of engagement to gain access to those things upon which you have now become dependent. Other nations will determine your behavior and your participation. It is a fact of life.

You cannot take your local universe by conquest because you will be opposed by everyone. This is a very different picture [from] your movies and your science fiction and your fantasies, your hopes and your unspoken expectations.

This casts a very different picture on the importance of human unity and cooperation here on Earth, the importance of securing and building human freedom and the power and presence of Knowledge that God has placed within each person.

Here freedom is not simply to become indulgent and unaccountable to anyone or anything else. It becomes an essential element of your participation in life. Here your greater gifts can be called forth, for you realize you are here to serve the great and imperiled needs of humanity. Here everything within you that is true and genuine becomes activated and called for.

Here nations will cease their endless conflicts and try to create stability for themselves and their neighbors to assure their future well-being and to protect themselves against intervention from the outside.

The world will not be taken by force, for that is not allowed in this part of the universe. It will be taken through seduction and persuasion, through capitalizing upon human weakness and conflict, human superstition and unfulfilled human needs.

Brute force is rarely used in this part of the universe. Greater, more subtle means are employed to protect the resources of the world and to gain ascendancy through persuasion, deception and secrecy. Humanity is still a clumsy, violent race in this regard, but even that is changing here on Earth.

We give you these perspectives because this represents the Love of the Creator. Though it might be overwhelming or frightening at first, it is a reality to which you must become aware and accustomed. You must think now not only for yourself or for your community or for your nation, but for the whole world because that will determine your fate and destiny, and the well-being of your children and the children of the world. It is a great shift in consciousness, a great and necessary shift now.

People will resist this, of course. They will take refuge in their religion. They will take refuge in their political ideology. They will take refuge in human rationality.

But life in the universe is not dependent upon these things. Life is happening whether you are aware of it or not, whether you are prepared for it or not. It is not a matter of perspective. It is not a matter of ideological orientation. It is really about paying attention, being observant and objective and honest with yourself.

This is a great challenge, but a necessary challenge, and a redeeming challenge if it can be met honestly and sincerely. You have the eyes to see and the ears to hear, but you are not looking and you are not listening.

Everyone around you seems to be obsessed, preoccupied or oppressed. Who will speak to them? Who will teach them? They may not hear Our words. Who will speak to them?

You need only point to the Revelation, for you yourself cannot explain life in the universe. You yourself cannot explain the Great Waves of change that are coming to the world. You yourself cannot explain what human spirituality means at the level of Knowledge. You yourself cannot explain Wisdom and Knowledge from the universe. You yourself cannot explain humanity's greater destiny and what must be done to achieve it.

For this you must turn to the Revelation, for the Revelation is greater than what any one person can understand. Point to the Revelation, for that alone holds the preparation for humanity's future and destiny in an emerging world.

God is giving humanity what it cannot give itself. God is alerting humanity to the perils and opportunities as it stands at the threshold of space. God is alerting humanity to the dangers and the opportunities and necessities of living in a declining world. God is bringing into the world a clarification of the nature and purpose of human spirituality, a nature and purpose that have been so lost and obscured in God's previous Revelations.

The Revelation is vast. It speaks of so many things. You cannot exhaust it, and you must use it and apply it and share its reality with others. It is only then that you will see what it really means and why it is necessary and why it holds the great promise for the future and the freedom of the people of this world.

For success is not assured. Many peoples in the universe have fallen under persuasion and subjugation. It has happened countless times. It is the inevitable outcome for people not being alerted and prepared to engage with a larger arena of intelligent life.

Beware of your own fantasies and expectations. Question them. Consider them in light of the realities of nature and of human history.

If you are honest with yourself, you must come to see that you do not know what is beyond the borders of this world, and that hopeful expectations can be extremely blinding. You must be prepared for anything and everything, just as you must be prepared for anything and everything functioning in this world in human relationships and through the activities of life itself.

To be free, you must be strong. To be strong, your mind must be clear. You must see clearly. You must hear the truth. You must be objective about your life and circumstances. You must look upon the world not with grievance or avoidance, but with compassion, patience and determination. If you are to forge the groundwork for a new future here, to play your small but important part here, then you must have this approach.

Accept this gift of love and Revelation. It brings with it great responsibility, but also great strength and great promise.

You are not living yet the life you were meant to live because your life is not engaged with the greater reality that lives within you and all around you. For humanity, this is a great turning point. And for you, it is a great turning point.

People of the world must awaken to the Greater Community and to the condition of the world you live in. You must learn of your greater strength and greater wisdom that God has placed within you to guide you, to prepare you and to protect you.

God has spoken again. It is for the greatest purpose to meet the greatest set of needs.

CHAPTER 5

WHO ARE THE ALLIES
OF HUMANITY?

As revealed to
Marshall Vian Summers
on February 3, 2011
in Seattle, Washington

Humanity is not alone in the universe, for the universe you will encounter is full of intelligent life. Living in a well-inhabited and long-established region of space, your world will find itself in a greater neighborhood.

Within this neighborhood are many powerful nations that have created vast networks of trade and commerce that are tightly governed. And most nations in this region of space are dependent upon these networks for the essential resources they need to support their technology and, in some cases, essential resources just to provide the basic requirements of life.

The world, therefore, is not in some remote and unexplored region of the universe. Your proximity to this great establishment of life gives you certain advantages and certain disadvantages.

Your advantage is that war and conquest are suppressed in this region of space. They are suppressed to maintain order and to provide security and stability for the larger networks of nations and their commerce and trade with one another. After going through long eras of war and competition and conflict, these larger networks have been established.

In this region of space, war is suppressed and outright conquest is not allowed. So if a nation wishes to gain advantage and influence in another world, such as an emerging world like your own, they must use more subtle means and employ other agents to carry out such an intervention.

You are facing, then, a non-human universe where freedom is rare, a universe that will seem foreign and even hostile to your presence should you escape the bounds of this solar system.

Here you will find that you have few friends and allies. But to your advantage, there is a network of free nations in this region of space who do not participate in these vast networks of trade and commerce. They have, over time and through great effort, established their insulation and their freedom to function [without] outside interference.

For it is always difficult for a free nation to exist around unfree nations. It is a delicate situation and has been an ongoing challenge for those free races whom you may consider to be the Allies of Humanity.

It is important to have this larger perspective. Otherwise, you will not understand what restrains your potential allies and why they are not interfering in the world today. They have, through secret means, sent an expedition to be near the Earth to witness the alien Intervention that is taking place here—an Intervention carried on by more unscrupulous races and organizations who seek to gain control of the world and its people through subtle and persuasive means.

Your Allies are here to provide wisdom and guidance and the perspective that humanity will need to comprehend the neighborhood of space into which you are emerging and what your advantages and disadvantages there are.

Indeed, there are great disadvantages because other worlds view your world with envy, and they see humanity in its warlike, divided state destroying the wealth and the value of this world. This, more than anything else, has led to the Intervention that is occurring here today.

[The Allies] expedition that is here [in the local universe] to observe this Intervention and to report on its activities and intentions is functioning here without the awareness of the free nations' governments. This is very important to understand. For these governments could be held accountable for the fact that humanity is gaining benefit from these free nations, which violates the agreements that the free nations have established—agreements of non-interference in the affairs of the Greater Community.

Such is the price they have had to pay to keep the Greater Community out of their regions and to avoid ongoing interference and attempts at persuasion that have plagued them for so very long.

It is for this reason that the Allies will not describe themselves, or give their names, or speak of their home worlds. For this expedition is functioning to serve humanity in secret, without the awareness or approval of greater powers, even without the awareness and approval, officially speaking, of the governments of their own nations.

It is a delicate situation. To understand this, you have to really consider the difficulty of establishing and maintaining freedom amongst greater powers where freedom is suppressed and avoided. It is a problem that humanity will have to face as it proceeds, as the human family emerges into a Greater Community of intelligent life.

How does a race such as yours maintain its freedom and self-determination amidst the presence of powerful and persuasive forces who will seek to undermine your confidence, your unity and your courage?

It is not a battle of weapons. It is not a battle of military might. It is a battle of will and intentions, a battle that is being played out [in] the mental environment—a great environment of influence where more powerful minds can influence weaker ones, an environment that humanity knows very little about.

The free nations in this part of the universe seek to promote freedom wherever they can. They view your world as showing great promise because spirituality and religion have not been destroyed or forgotten here. They see that the power of Knowledge, the greater spiritual power, is still alive in individuals, despite humanity's grave mistakes and foolish activities.

The Allies of Humanity have sent a series of Briefings into the world to advise and to prepare humanity for its engagement with the Greater Community. These Briefings present information that no one on Earth could create or know for themselves. They create a perspective that humanity does not presently have regarding the prospects for contact and the consequences of contact.

The Briefings correct many of humanity's false assumptions and uninformed beliefs—assumptions and beliefs that make you vulnerable to foreign manipulation and persuasion. The Briefings themselves encourage humanity's independence in the universe and the importance of not allowing foreign nations to establish their interests here and foster dependence upon their foreign technology.

This is a great service to an unwary and unsuspecting humanity, who believes the universe is either a great empty place awaiting exploration or that it is filled with benign and ethical races of beings who would be eager to assist humanity in its quest for technological solutions and greater power.

This naïve and foolish perspective, of course, means that you are uninformed and uneducated about the realities of life beyond your borders. You still think that technology can overcome the power of nature.

The Allies of Humanity Briefings, along with God's New Revelation for humanity—the New Message for humanity—will give you a much clearer and more correct understanding. For you need this if you are to proceed with wisdom, caution and discernment.

After the publication of the first set of the Briefings from the Allies of Humanity, the Allies' position in this solar system was discovered, and they were forced to flee. Now they have to report from a hidden location far beyond your solar system.

In the third set of The Allies of Humanity Briefings, they are speaking about the realities of life—of trade and commerce, interaction that exists in your neighborhood of space—and the requirements for freedom that humanity will have to foster and support if it is to remain self-sufficient and self-determined in a Greater Community of life.

It is important for you to understand that the Creator of all life, through the Angelic Presence, has called upon these free races to provide this assistance to humanity. They are here and guided by a Divine mission, the expedition itself.

The governments of the free nations will claim no knowledge of this expedition, for they have very little knowledge of it. This is being guided by a greater force and set of Powers in the universe—Spiritual Powers serving the Creator of all life, seeking to support freedom wherever it can be established.

It is important for you to understand also that the Allies of Humanity have a debt to pay, for they were served by an expedition in an earlier time that helped to free them from the grip of intervention, opening the way for them to establish their freedom and autonomy in the universe. They now have an opportunity to repay this debt by providing a similar service to humanity, as you yourselves face intervention and all of the dangers and misfortune it can bring.

Humanity knows not of its vulnerability in space. You still think the universe is there to serve you, that you are special and that anyone who would come here would come here seeking to assist you, to enlighten you or to save you from your own errors. Such are the misconceptions of an isolated race, who has never had to adapt itself to the realities of the Greater Community.

Therefore, great assistance is being brought to humanity—great assistance providing wisdom and knowledge that humanity cannot provide for itself, great assistance that has been prompted by the Will of the Creator and carried out by certain individuals from several different worlds. It is an expedition that has been very dangerous for its participants and has taken a great deal of time.

Therefore, when you begin to study the Briefings from the Allies of Humanity, it is important to consider the risks that have been taken to provide this wisdom and the immense importance of the wisdom and perspective that are provided in these teachings.

Take them to heart and think of them deeply. Ask your questions, but understand that you are at the very beginning of your Greater Community education and you will have to live with certain questions that cannot yet be answered, building while you proceed a growing and concise understanding of humanity's advantages and disadvantages.

There are many sets of eyes watching the world at this time. That is part of your disadvantage. But military conquest will not be sought here because the world is too valuable, and the foreign races who seek to establish themselves here need humanity as their workforce—a compliant and willing workforce—for these foreign races cannot live in this environment, for reasons that you would not guess.

It is a situation that must be understood correctly, which requires a great deal of information and perspective and a correction of many ideas that are prevalent still in the world today.

One person has been chosen to receive the Allies of Humanity Briefings. He is the individual who is also receiving God's New Revelation to prepare humanity for the great change that is coming to the environments of the world and for humanity's encounter with the Greater Community itself. He has been guided by the Lord of the universe through the Angelic Presence, and he has also been the recipient of the Allies of Humanity Briefings, Briefings which have been guided and prompted by the Lord of the universe through the Angelic Presence.

You must see that this had to come through one person who was sent into the world for this purpose, to serve this role. Otherwise, the message would become contaminated, and it would certainly become lost if it were given to more than one individual, with many different versions and interpretations.

It has taken the Messenger decades to prepare to receive the New Message and to receive the Allies of Humanity Briefings. The Briefings themselves were received on very distinct dates, with long periods of time intervening where no contact occurred at all.

The Briefings were made available with the assistance of the Angelic Presence, being communicated through a spiritual means that did not require the use of technology, a means of communication that the Intervention itself could not intercept or interpret. Again, this was done to protect the location of the Allies' expedition, as well as the purity and integrity of the message itself.

We give you this perspective and this background so that you may understand the significance and the nature of the communications that are being sent to the world today from those free nations that exist in your region of space.

It is not an easy thing to consider because there are other messages being sent to the world at this time—messages from the Intervention, speaking of the nobility of their presence here and humanity's dependence upon their guidance and their wisdom, speaking of lofty beings and great kingdoms and establishments and a network of wealth and prosperity that humanity is encouraged to become a part of.

These are the seductions and inducements of the unfree nations, speaking to humanity's fears and ambitions. Many people have fallen under this persuasion. Many individuals in leadership positions of governments and commerce and religion are swayed by such things, being promised tremendous power, tremendous wealth and advantage.

Within the Allies of Humanity Briefings, you will hear a very different presentation, one that speaks to humanity's inherent strength, courage and ability. It will advise humanity not to receive any technology from the Greater Community, for it is only being offered to develop dependence—dependence upon foreign powers and the great networks of trade. Once you become dependent upon these things for your technology or basic requirements, your freedom will be lost, and you will be governed from afar to meet the terms of engagement.

It takes great heart to face these things, but face them you must, for this is your world. Your isolation in the universe is over. From here on, there will be attempts at persuasion and intervention. The Allies will not intervene here. They will not establish bases in the world or try to manipulate human perception or seduce leaders of government, commerce or religion. They know that humanity must gain [its] freedom on its own, without outside control and manipulation.

This is a dangerous time for humanity, for your resources are declining, and your climate is becoming ever more unstable. Your environment is deteriorating. Ever greater numbers of people are drinking from a slowly shrinking well.

This is a dangerous time for humanity, for you are vulnerable to persuasion and manipulation and deception, knowing little or nothing about the realities of life in the universe or how your freedom must be sustained and defended as you emerge into this larger arena of life.

The Allies of Humanity seek no relations with humanity because they recognize humanity is not ready for contact. Humanity does not have the maturity, the unity or the discernment yet to tell friend from foe and to understand the complexities of life where thousands of races are interacting with each other.

If you think of this for a moment and imagine how difficult it is to establish agreements or negotiations with races that think differently, look different and have different concepts, different histories, different priorities, it would make your human negotiations seem simple and obvious in comparison.

It is a vast and complicated situation, and you must grow up to participate in this universe of life. You cannot be adolescent and destructive and aggressive, for you will find yourself alone, with great opposition around you.

For humanity to be self-sufficient and a sovereign race, free from outside governance and control, you must then follow what the Allies Briefings are providing for you. The Allies will not come to save humanity from intervention through the use of force or military means, for this would destroy their autonomy in the universe, which they have taken centuries to establish.

They give you the wisdom that you cannot not give yourself. They give you the perspective you cannot give yourself. They give you the information you cannot gain yourself. It is now up to humanity, the strength of humanity, the integrity of humanity and humanity's native wisdom to teach you how to offset the Intervention and to build your capacity and your strength as a free race.

This would mean the cessation of conflict in the world and a far greater cooperation between nations than currently exists, or that has ever existed. What will be the impetus for this but the threat of facing a universe where freedom is rare and where many are looking at the world with envy?

You do not realize what a prize this world is and why other nations would intervene here to try to save it for themselves, using humanity as but a resource in and of itself.

It is time for you to grow up and think of greater things—to think of the welfare of your planet, to think of the stability of your environment, to think of world security now and not merely the security of your own nation.

This is a great opportunity for human unity, perhaps the greatest you will ever have. For the need is the greatest you will ever face, and the challenge is the greatest you have ever encountered.

It is a situation that requires courage and objectivity, the willingness to learn things you have never learned before and the willingness to realize what humanity has learned through its long and difficult history regarding intervention and the dangers to the freedom and self-determination of the native peoples.

All of humanity are now the native peoples of the world facing Intervention—an Intervention that is here to use you for itself, for its own wealth and acquisition.

You do not realize the biological wealth of this world, and the resources that exist within the complex web of life here that are sought after and valued in a universe of barren planets.

There is so much for humanity to learn. That is why God has sent a New Revelation into the world and has called upon the Allies of Humanity to provide their wisdom and their counsel to assist in this great effort to educate humanity and to alert humanity about the great dangers and opportunities that exist as it stands at the threshold of space.

The Revelation of the New Message and the importance of the Allies of Humanity Briefings should not be underestimated. They represent the most important documents in the world today and the greatest needs facing humanity, which are still unknown to so many.

You are fortunate to receive this. You are blessed to receive this. Proceed now with a courageous heart, and allow yourself to receive the gift of love from the Creator of all life and the reassurance that you have other races in the universe who support humanity's freedom and independence. In time, you will come to depend on these two great sources of comfort as never before.

The power and the presence of Knowledge that lives within each person is the greater intelligence within the individual. It is this greater intelligence that the New Message speaks to and speaks of. It is this greater intelligence that the Allies of Humanity expedition is attempting to ignite and to communicate to you.

This holds the secrets of humanity's spirituality and the promise of your greater destiny in the universe—a destiny as a free and self-determined peoples. But your destiny is not assured. The outcome is uncertain. You as an individual must have great faith in the power of Knowledge within yourself and within others to turn the tide in humanity's favor.

The risk to humanity's freedom in the universe and the decline of the world that you live in are the two great motivations for human freedom and unity, for humanity's wisdom and greater cooperation.

But these two threatening realities can also lead humanity into conflict, war and deprivation, leading to certain subjugation to foreign powers. So the risks are great, and the rewards of choosing correctly are immense, paving the way for a greater future for the human family.

Let this be your understanding.

CHAPTER 6

THE ENEMIES OF HUMANITY

As revealed to
Marshall Vian Summers
on May 24, 2014
in Boulder, Colorado

Humanity has enemies in the universe. They are not opposed to you, but they seek what you have. They seek to take what you have from you without the use of undue force, relying upon the powers of persuasion and sowing the seeds of division amongst a contentious humanity.

They seek this world for themselves. They do not seek to destroy you, but to use you as a workforce for them. It is something very subtle in its application, but very real in its effect.

They are competitors for the world, this precious world, such a rare gem in the universe. You have no idea how rare it is and how valuable it is to so many races who would seek to use its biological and mineral wealth for their own purposes. You are like the native tribe being discovered by the outside world, of which you know nothing about.

The intruders will not seek conquest outright, but a willful submission on your part. Once you have depleted this world sufficiently; once you have altered the climate of the world sufficiently; once you have destroyed civilization sufficiently through conflict, competition and war, they will arrive. They are here already—furthering human conflict, sowing the seeds of your undoing, not to crush you, but to have you submit.

This is how intelligent races gain control of worlds that are stewarded by races who are less intelligent and who are conflicted amongst themselves. The use of force is not employed because it would destroy the very assets of the world and would destroy humanity as a workforce.

For those who seek your world cannot live here. They cannot breathe your atmosphere. They are unprotected against the biological contamination of the world. They need you, and they will offer you anything they can as an inducement for you to allow them to guide you—promising to save you from your great and ever-growing calamity, promising to give you peace and equanimity, freedom from war and conflict, saying that they themselves have no war. And yet it is all but a deception, you see.

It is all a powerful deception, given to an unsuspecting humanity—a humanity that is mesmerized by its newfound technology and who will be so impressed by demonstrations of technology at a greater level; a humanity that is desperate for answers to the Great Waves of change that are coming to the world; a humanity that seeks power and wealth even as it depletes its own world beyond recognition.

You must come to understand this, or you will think the universe is just a big empty place for you to explore, and to get whatever you want, and to replace whatever you have destroyed or consumed here on Earth. You will think you are special in this universe and that other races will come to help you because you are so special. You [will] think the universe runs according to your philosophy, to your religious understanding, to your ethics, to your concepts—you who know nothing about this Greater Community of life in which you live.

THE ENEMIES OF HUMANITY

Humanity stands at great peril here, extremely vulnerable, destroying relentlessly your self-sufficiency in this world, which invites intervention from beyond: an opportunity to make humanity dependent upon foreign powers, to gain control of this world without the use of force, to conquer the world without the usual methods of conquest that humanity assumes and still employs.

There are only two things that could unite the human family. It is environmental collapse or it is competition from beyond. Both are happening now, one more apparently than the other. [Yet] they are both underway. You cannot stop them entirely until you have gained a greater strength individually and collectively. If this were understood, war would end tomorrow. War would end tomorrow, and the avenues of cooperation would be established for everyone's survival, freedom and benefit.

People do not want to hear these things, for they would feel helpless and hopeless immediately, having no sense of their real strength and having lost confidence in their leaders and governments and institutions.

Humanity has now established an infrastructure that foreign races can utilize. That is why intervention of this nature has never occurred before. Humanity has global communications, global commerce. It has taken control of the world sufficiently that another race can step in to take advantage of your accomplishments and your development.

Even at this moment, people are being turned to the Intervention— to serve it, believing it will bring peace and equanimity to a world of escalating uncertainty and discord. Already, the Intervention is gaining adherents and representatives, thinking they [the Intervention] are representing some kind of enlightened force from beyond the world, when in fact they are only competitors seeking to take advantage of the world.

The Intervention does not have military assets. It relies upon persuasion and dissension to gain control. It does this because conquest is not allowed in this part of the universe, a reality that you know nothing about. Besides, advanced races have found other ways to gain access to the resources of the universe without the use of force.

People are being taken against their will. Some of them are never returned. They are being used for experimentation, to create hybrids, those who look like human beings but who are united with the Intervention. It is a hideous project. It is dangerous. It is being fostered by the enemies of humanity.

Those who seek domination here have no value for your freedom. They are not interested in your concepts. They think you are primitive. They think you are destructive. They think you are out of control.

They think you are ridiculous because of all the transmissions that continue to be sent out into the universe, portraying humanity as a race that is destructive, violent and indulgent. It is the worst kind of representation of the real merit and spirit of humanity, and yet that is what you are presenting to the universe, and have been presenting to the universe for decades and decades.

You think you live in isolation in the universe. Even your scientists think that no one can get here, as if the entire universe is limited by humanity's scientific understanding.

You assume you have special importance in this universe. You think that any visitation would be beneficial to you. But the history of intervention in your own world proves otherwise. Visitors arrive for their own purposes—to gain resources, to gain land and property. They seek to conquer in all cases. This has been the history of intervention in your world, and so do not assume it is different in the universe.

The true Allies of Humanity would never do these things. They would only send their wisdom and their warning, which they have already done in a series of Briefings for the human family.

Intervention is unethical. It is corrupting. It is circumventing the power and authority of the native people. It is usurpation in its most deceptive form.

Do not be persuaded. Do not be beguiled by an advanced technology. Do not think that those in the universe are not driven by the same needs that drive the human family. For advanced societies everywhere are in desperate pursuit of resources and must trade and barter and travel great distances to achieve what they need. It is a complex situation, of which humanity knows nothing at all.

The Lord of the universe has sent a great preparation to Earth to prepare humanity to face a declining world, a world of diminishing resources and violent weather in a changing environment.

The Lord of the universe has sent a preparation for this Greater Community, and a great warning about the Intervention that is already underway in the world today and its power over people's ideas and perspective and attitudes. Only the Lord of the universe would know how to prepare humanity for the Greater Community, for only the Lord of the universe knows the heart and the soul of each person and of humanity as a whole.

This is the great challenge, operating on two fronts. The first is the threat of disintegration internally as humanity now begins to undermine its own well-being in its natural world. The second is intervention from the universe beyond, which often happens under these circumstances. For it is a great opportunity for a foreign race to establish its influence and power in a world undergoing the kind of change that humanity is now facing. It has happened countless times in the history of the universe.

It is a great warning, but humanity has the power to thwart intervention once it learns how the universe around it really works. God has provided this insight, revealing for the first time what life in the universe really looks like, how it functions and what one must do to become free in a universe where freedom is rare.

It is the perfect Revelation for humanity standing at the threshold of space, facing the Great Waves of change in the world. It is a gift of such Grace and the great Love for humanity.

Here the ancient Revelations cannot prepare you, for they were not designed for this. They cannot give you strength, courage, wisdom and power here, for they were not designed for this.

Humanity has arrived at a whole new turning point, a great threshold—the greatest threshold that any intelligent race will face in the universe—as it faces environmental decline at home and intervention from beyond.

There is so much for you to learn here. There are so many questions that you will need to ask, and most of them can be answered through

God's Revelation for the world. For God is here to prepare humanity for this Greater Community. God is here to further humanity's freedom and unity in this world. God is here to provide what humanity will need to maintain its sovereignty here and to build a future, a better future than its past.

But to have this future, you will have to face these two great challenges to the human family. Greater they are than anything that has ever happened in the world before. It is not something that government leaders alone can deal with. It will require the support and awareness of people everywhere.

But the hour is late, and only now are the Great Waves of change coming to the world beginning to become apparent to more and more people. Only now the hidden reality of intervention is beginning to be recognized by enough people that this Revelation can be recognized and understood.

Yet the hour is late. Humanity does not have much time to prepare. Every year is significant. Every life is important. Every person has purpose and meaning, for you have all come to face the world and to serve the world under these very conditions that We speak of here today.

You will be fighting a battle on two fronts: a battle to preserve the world and to offset the damage that has already been done to the stability of this world; and you will be warding off intervention, making public all of its demonstrations in the world.

It is not a battle between armies. It is a battle of will and purpose; a battle of determination; a battle of awareness, clarity and objectivity against opposing forces who have already prepared for the

Intervention here. They know much more about you than you know about them.

Here enough people must become strong and resistant to this if humanity is going to preserve its freedom into the future. Therefore, you are entering a great age of unity and cooperation. That is the next great work of the human family—to preserve the world and to protect its freedom from foreign intervention and persuasion.

Do not accept gifts from the Intervention, for they are only here to seduce you. Do not accept promises of peace, power and equanimity or spiritual fulfillment, for such promises are empty and are only here to seduce you. Do not acquiesce and think that humanity is hopeless without this Intervention, for that is not true, and that will only serve those who oppose you and who will take from you everything that you have. Do not think that humanity cannot preserve itself here, for it has many advantages in the universe of which it is unaware.

God's Revelation reveals what these are for the first time. It is important that you know of this. It is important that you not lose heart or become jaded or cynical or think that you can do nothing, for that is the Intervention's persuasion.

You must see these things now and know these things if you are to understand what is really happening in the world today, the great threat facing the human family and the great possibility and promise this gives for human unity and cooperation to finally be established, which can only be established in the face of great difficulty and a great challenge.

Here every person must participate. Every person must become aware to some extent. Every person must realize that it is not their national security that is at risk. It is the security of the whole world.

You cannot afford to have nations fail and collapse now, or fall under the persuasion of the Intervention, for that would surely generate great war and conflict across the globe. For it is in the Intervention's interests that humanity fight itself, defeat itself and diminish itself. They will not fight you directly in this way.

It is cunning. It has been used countless times before, but not always with success. For races that resist can prevail. Races that realize their great challenge will prevail. Nations that value their world, recognizing the danger that is upon them, will prevail.

Here your greater strengths will be called for from you. Here your weakness and foolish indulgences and pathetic self-recrimination can be escaped because you are called into a greater service, a greater need and a greater unity in the human family.

What else could overcome centuries-old animosity between nations, cultures and religions but a greater threat that seems to overwhelm all and threaten all equally?

There is redemption here if you can see it, if you can realize it, if you have the heart and the courage to face it and to learn what it really means and how humanity can prevail—both within this world and from Intervention from beyond.

It is a challenge that can restore the human family and give it a greater future of unity, purpose and power that is far beyond anything it has ever been able to establish before.

God's New Revelation for the world brings the warning, the blessing and the preparation. It is more comprehensive than anything that has ever been given to this world, speaking now to a literate world, a world of global commerce and communication.

It is the only thing in the world that can save the human family, for it reveals the great danger that is occurring, from within and from beyond. And only it can provide the wisdom necessary to overcome these great challenges and to restore to each individual and to humanity as a whole the strength, power and purpose that are its birthright and promise.

CHAPTER 7

HUMANITY'S DESTINY IN THE GREATER COMMUNITY

As revealed to
Marshall Vian Summers
on July 21, 2007
in Boulder, Colorado

Humanity and the world stand at the threshold of the greatest change it will ever encounter. This change will be wrought in part by humanity's misuse of the world and humanity's impact upon the natural environment of the world. But included in this is the Intervention from races from beyond the world who seek to take advantage of a weak and divided humanity.

These two great events, these two great phenomena, are directly connected. For those who seek to intervene in the world seek to have humanity become weak and divided and to have you plunge into conflict—your nations struggling over the remaining resources; your nations fighting with each other for food, water and energy rights and access.

Into an increasingly chaotic situation, those who are intervening in the world, who rely upon mental persuasion above all else to achieve their goals, will present themselves as the saviors of humanity. They will come with their advanced technology, proclaiming that they do not have war, that they do not have conflict, that they have learned to live in peace and equanimity.

But their presentation, as convincing as it may sound, is entirely a deception. For they are nothing more than resource explorers and commercial interests who seek to gain control of the world and the world's people.

They do not have military strength. That is not their power. They do not have vast armies. They are not going to come and take the world by force, for this they cannot do. Instead, their strength is more subtle and more pervasive and, in the end, far more successful than any use of force would be.

Humanity's destiny is to emerge into a Greater Community of intelligent life in the universe. The Greater Community represents races and nations of beings at all levels of evolution, representing an immense diversity of life. But at present humanity knows nothing of the Greater Community. You only have your wishes and your fears and your aspirations to fill in the great question of what exists beyond your borders.

What exists beyond your borders is a competitive environment, unlike anything you can possibly imagine. Here there are races that are mature. Here there are races that have learned how to gain what they need without the use of weapons and force. Here races have realized that the strength and the power of the mind in the mental environment is far more effective and far more constructive than trying to exert influence through weaponry or by physical force.

Humanity only has an inkling of what this greater power may be, and [yet] indeed this greater power is known to you. It is power and influence in the mental environment. In the simplest of forms, it is represented by a parent's influence over their children, or a government's influence over their people, or a merchant's influence over his or her customers. Trying to persuade people to do what you

want them to do and to not do what you do not want them to do; to
persuade them to be compliant, to pacify them, to direct them and to
control them.

While this influence in the mental environment has very positive
applications, what you are facing in the Greater Community poses
the greatest threat to human freedom and sovereignty in this world.
This threat is even greater than environmental decline and the
wasting of your resources. Though such things will have immense
consequence on the quality of life and the quantity of life within your
human family, your encountering the Interventions from beyond the
world has far greater consequences for the future and the destiny of
the human family.

At present, even your most educated people still think you live
in isolation, that perhaps there is intelligent life somewhere in
the universe, but it is assumed that no one can get here, as if the
entire universe is limited by the boundaries of human science
and understanding.

Indeed, you have lived in isolation for so long that it represents the
entire context of your understanding of yourself—the context
for your philosophies, your religions, your theology and your
social structures.

To encounter, then, the Greater Community—particularly forces
from the Greater Community who seek to intervene in your world
for their own purposes—represents not only a great threat to your
freedom, but also a great shock to your awareness, to your beliefs and
to your assumptions.

Even your belief about God will have to go through a radical change
here, for whether you realize it or not, God—or the Source of all

life—is always considered within a human context. [God] is believed to represent human values and aspirations, human tendencies.

Sometimes this is made into a physical image of God as a human being. But whether this be the case or not, God is supposed, by people on Earth, to demonstrate human qualities and human virtues.

But when you consider a God of the entire Greater Community—of this galaxy and other galaxies, representing countless races of beings who are so different from you, whose beliefs and values are so different from yours, whose physical appearance and whose social structures are so unique and different from yours—this is why there is a psychic barrier, a barrier of belief against recognizing the presence of the Intervention in the world today and what it portends for humanity's future and humanity's freedom.

While it is true that humanity has potential allies in the local universe, it is even more important to realize that your first encounter with intelligent life will not be with saints and environmentalists, but with resource explorers and economic collectives—groups that search and travel to gain access to resources and to planets of biological and strategic importance.

In a sense, they represent the "scavenger" races even though they are technologically far advanced of you and have a very rigid social structure. Nonetheless, they are out to explore and to exploit in contrast to most settled nations—who have established a degree of stability, who do not travel into deep space looking for resources necessarily, who maintain their insulation and their isolation with great emphasis and great discretion.

The scavenger races instead seek to explore and exploit anything they can. And your beautiful world—with its splendid biological diversity, with its immense strategic importance, and with important [artifacts] from its ancient history—represents an irresistible goal, an irresistible asset for such races as these. And there are more than one. In fact, each group, or collective, represents many races established in a very hierarchical pattern.

So while a few people in the world today dream about the glory and the splendor of contact, plans are being laid, foundations are being built and influence is being cast to prepare humanity to fall under a greater persuasion. This persuasion will encourage competition and conflict in the world. It will emphasize and encourage nations to struggle and fight for what they need and what they want, which will be an ever-increasing emphasis in a world of declining resources and growing populations.

And because humanity is so completely self-obsessed and people have so little awareness of the Greater Community—even that there is a Greater Community—humanity is remarkably susceptible and vulnerable to such forms of persuasion.

Even today, within certain religious circles, great persuasion is being cast so that religious leaders, if they are aware of the Greater Community reality at all, will tend to think that foreign visitors must be ethically and morally superior to humanity.

This reckless assumption is growing in the world amongst religious leaders, and it is supplanted by humanity's hope that there is a better life somewhere else than what is being experienced here today—the desire to be saved, the desire to be rescued, the desire to be guided, the desire to be protected.

So today you have this focus on surrender, on acquiescence, on acceptance. And so your critical faculties are not developed and are not applied. You become less wary. You become less objective. You become less perceptive. You are encouraged to immerse yourself in your own internal questions and conflicts and take your eyes off your environment and your surroundings.

This is not merely an accident. It is not merely the result of affluent living. It is not merely human nature alone that accounts for this great change in human awareness and human emphasis.

Even those who are wary and observant are far more concerned about what other tribes of people are doing or might do. Who is watching your boundary to space? Who is encouraged to watch your boundaries to space?

Think of the native peoples who allowed intervention to take place. Consider what happened there. It is a situation that has been repeated many times within your world and countless times within the Greater Community.

For the strong will dominate the weak if they can. It is true here in this world. It is true in the Greater Community.

At present, people think the Greater Community is just this great empty place that humanity will explore and exploit for its own needs. But once you move beyond your solar system, then you are entering territories that are owned by others, and the resources that you might seek for yourself once you are able to travel in this manner, these resources will be owned by others.

But it is unlikely that humanity will even reach such a point of contact or exploration because your first encounters with the Greater Community will be with resource explorers, with scavenger races, with those who will seek to take advantage of your superstitions, your ignorance, your obsessions and your conflicts with one another.

Their goal and purpose here is to gain access to the biological resources of the world and the strategic position of the world. They are not interested in you. They see you as being chaotic and unruly and far inferior to them. As it is the custom, conquerors always feel that those that they wish to subjugate are inferior to them.

Indeed, the Intervention that is functioning in the world today will encourage this sense of inferiority. They will encourage people to lose their awareness of humanity's value and purpose. They will discourage these things. They will discourage your self-confidence, your self-trust and your confidence and trust in the human family, creating a vacuum of confidence that they then can fulfill.

Therefore, your contact with the Greater Community is not some distant future event when you finally gain the technological ability to travel into space. Your confrontation with the Greater Community is occurring now. It is not what you think. You are the native peoples of this world. You are being exploited. Intervention is underway and has been for decades.

The New Message from God speaks of this, reveals this and warns of this. It is the greatest event in human history. It is the greatest threat and danger to human freedom and sovereignty in this world. And yet it represents the greatest chance, and the greatest possibility, and the greatest need for human unity and cooperation.

This unity and cooperation are necessary to prevent further decline in the world's resources, for if humanity loses its self-sufficiency in the Greater Community, you will surely lose your freedom and self-determination. You will force the world into such a state of decline that you will accept whatever the Intervention offers you. You will not be in a position to negotiate favorable terms for yourself.

For your needs will be oppressing and overwhelming. You will extend trust where it should not be extended, and you will accept technology that should not be accepted. You will give over authority where it should not be given over. And you will become dependent on those who supply you with those things that you now need and cannot question.

You need human unity and cooperation to prevent further decline in the world, for you are living now in a world in decline. You also need human unity and cooperation for the defense of the world. It is not national security now. It is the security of the world.

You take for granted your position of superiority in this world. You take advantage and assume that your place in this world is a God-given right, that it is unchallenged and that it is something that you can be assured of, as if it were an entitlement of some kind.

But freedom must be defended. Such freedom and sovereignty is rare in the Greater Community. There are far more nations that have been conquered and absorbed into larger empires than there are independent worlds.

To have independence and freedom in the Greater Community, you must be self-sufficient, you must be united, and you must be extremely discreet. Included in this is that you must be vigilant about protecting your borders, as vigilant as you would be about [preventing] someone [from] entering your home, a stranger in your home.

Yet at this moment, such vigilance is not exercised. Such discretion is not exercised. Human unity does not yet exist. The only advantage you have at this point is your self-sufficiency, and you are in the process of destroying even that.

If humanity understood its position in the universe and understood the nature of the reality beyond your borders, you would not allow any foreigner to set foot in this world without the expressed permission of the people of this world. You would be extremely careful about who can enter here and what they can do in your world.

But at present the Intervention functions at will. It travels at will. It takes people against their will. It exploits people. It changes people. It destroys people. It is fundamentally evil.

Some people will say, "Well, what can we do against such great powers?" But the Intervention is small. It has no military assets to speak of. It is relying completely on human belief and acquiescence. It is relying upon its influence over human tendencies and human weakness. In the face of human strength, it has little efficacy.

Part of the purpose of the New Message from God and its great warning for humanity is to generate this strength and this awareness. For you must be extremely wary in the Greater Community, for you have reached a point in your own development where others can take advantage of your technology, your planetary commerce and communication.

Intervening races do not want to see you gain greater technological power, or intervention here will become far more difficult. So this now is the great opportunity. Before humanity can unite, before humanity gains greater power and greater weaponry, before humanity realizes its own position, Intervention will be and is being attempted here.

Therefore, you see, your destiny is upon you. It is here now. It is not some future possibility. It does not merely depend upon perspective on your part. It is the greater reality that is occurring in the world, and people are unaware and are not responding.

If governments know, they do not share their information with their own populations. And religious leaders are either completely ignorant or are falling under persuasion.

It is what you cannot see now that has the greatest threat to you. It is what you do not recognize in your daily life that has the power to change your circumstances utterly and forever. For if humanity loses its freedom and its self-determination in this world, the chances of your ever having it again are very small.

To understand the meaning, and the grace, and the power and the efficacy of God's New Message, and the purpose for it being given to the world at this time, you must recognize the great threat, the Greater Darkness that is in the world.

You must reverse the decline of the world, and you must protect yourself against the Greater Community. Both will require greater human unity and cooperation. Both are extremely compelling once you recognize them.

For what can any nation in this world gain, what advantage can it secure for itself if the whole world will lose its freedom and fall under subjugation? And do not think that such subjugation will be an improvement over your current circumstances, for that would be a fatal error on your part.

HUMANITY'S DESTINY IN THE
GREATER COMMUNITY

Your potential rulers would treat humanity no better than you treat your domestic animals today. They do not regard you as their equals, and they are not interested in your fascinating qualities. And they do not understand your spirituality, except insofar that it can be used against you to weaken you, to disarm you and to distract you.

Such forces do not know of the sacred Knowledge that exists within all intelligent life, for if they did, they would not be intervening in the world. They would not be seeking to conquer and to subjugate the human family.

For this sacred Knowledge is rare. To gain greater technology does not mean that you gain awareness of this sacred Knowledge. It only means you gain greater technology.

There are so many things that humanity must reconsider, that you must reconsider, that you will need to become aware of. For at the moment, you have great reactions to problems that are small and little reaction to problems that are great.

You do not see that your destiny is determining and will determine everything, that the Greater Community is the greatest event in human history and will require the greatest degree of human unity and cooperation that have ever been established in the world before. For everyone will be in the same boat now. No nation has any advantage regarding the Intervention. You are all resources to be explored and exploited.

If you can consider this, if you can bring greater objectivity to your understanding here, you will begin to see how compelling and how necessary human unity and cooperation is. It is not simply a good idea. It is not simply a virtue. It is not simply a preferred manner of functioning. It is necessary for your survival, for your freedom and for your future. That is how significant this is.

Consider the native peoples of the world. One day their life was always as it had been for centuries, or even millennia. The next day, everything begins to change and to collapse. And what changes one day from another here is intervention.

Intervention is part of nature. Competition for environment is part of nature. Do not think that great and complex technology lifts people above these powers and these forces in nature. And do not think that because you seem to have a pre-eminent position in the world and assume that this pre-eminence is permanent, that you have any power or efficacy in the Greater Community.

Even your neighbors, who do not intervene here, do not hold you with much respect. You are clearly destructive, aggressive and competitive. Even your neighbors who have visited the world before to observe you, but who do not now intervene, do not have respect for the human family.

You have not yet become respectable. You are not stable. You are not united. And you treat this world, which is a magnificent planet, in such a reckless and shortsighted manner.

Races that have established permanence and stability in the Greater Community certainly do not behave in such a way. And whatever resources they still have in their worlds are protected and sustained and maintained with great determination.

If you can hear these words, which represent part of a New Message from God, then you can begin to see with greater eyes, see the big picture of your life and the life of humanity. You can begin to see the

great strength that the Creator of all life has placed within the human
family, within each heart: the sacred Knowledge. And you can begin
to see the great predicament that humanity is creating for itself and
also allowing to occur here.

The New Message from God will reveal this in far greater detail,
but you must be alerted, you must be warned, and you must be
prepared. And who in the world can do this? Who in the world
understands what is going on in the Greater Community? Who in the
world knows who is intervening here, why they are here, what their
methods are and what they intend to do? Who in the world knows
humanity's ancient history and the prospects for its future?

Clearly, such Wisdom and Knowledge must come from God. For
there is no person in the world who could have such Knowledge and
Wisdom unless God gave it to them, unless it has been revealed in a
New Message from God, not for one person, not for some elite group,
not for one government alone, not for one religious leader, but for the
whole of humanity—a New Message from God for the protection and
advancement of humanity.

For what has been provided to humanity thus far in God's great
[Messages] cannot prepare you now for the Greater Community.
It represents an entirely new reality, a complete shift in your
circumstances. It requires a New Message from God.

While ancient wisdom is embedded in all the great religious
traditions, none of them can prepare you for what you must do now.
And that is why there is a New Message from God—not to compete
with the world's religions, not to overshadow them, but to unite them
and to strengthen them so that their ancient wisdom can come to the

fore and serve humanity in its changing circumstances at this great threshold in your evolution.

In hearing these words, your mind may object. Your mind may question. Your mind may doubt. Your mind may compare and contrast. But in your heart, you will know.

If you do not know your own heart, then you do not know what you know. If you do not know and are not aware of the wisdom that God has placed within you, then you will not know what you know. You will only be aware of what you think. And this is the condition of the vast majority of people in the world today.

So while you are facing the greatest challenge and the greatest threshold in your history, what is also being called for is this sacred Knowledge to emerge in many more people. There must be many more eyes looking. There must be greater objectivity. There must be greater clarity.

This wisdom that God has placed within you is not in competition with itself or in conflict with itself [in others]. It, therefore, represents the greatest force for unity, and peace and cooperation that is possible in this world or in any world.

This sacred Knowledge is a calling from God. It is here to guide you, to protect you and to lead you to a greater contribution to a world in need, which will fulfill the needs of your soul.

You do not know the need of your soul yet. The world must reveal it to you. Do not seek for comfort and consolation. Do not seek to run and escape. For you will never meet the need of your soul if you do this.

HUMANITY'S DESTINY IN THE
GREATER COMMUNITY

Your gifts are meant for certain people and certain situations. Knowledge will take you there. Knowledge will lead you there. It will not be your wishes and your fears and your preferences. It will be Knowledge.

You need this Knowledge to be fulfilled and to be complete and to satisfy the deeper needs of your soul. And the world needs your contribution, for without it, the future of humanity becomes less certain and more grave.

The possibility for humans, for humanity's success in emerging into the Greater Community as a free and sovereign race, will depend on the contribution of many people. This contribution resides within Knowledge within them.

Therefore, the New Message from God must provide the way to Knowledge and the calling for Knowledge. It is not simply a belief system to be compared with other belief systems. It is not simply a different point of view or perspective.

Do not be foolish and think like this. It is the answer. And it is the answer for a problem you have not even yet recognized and for which you are not yet prepared.

What is human destiny? Human destiny is in the Greater Community. But you must survive your emergence into the Greater Community. And you must survive competition from the Greater Community if you are to be able to function there.

For your isolation is over, and you will never have it again. From this moment forward, you must build and protect human freedom and sovereignty in this world. You must protect the resources of this world and your self-sufficiency here. And you must gain the wisdom to discern friend from foe, ally from competitor.

You do not have this wisdom and this discernment yet, but it can and must grow within you as an individual and within the human family.

Do not think that humanity does not have promise here, for to do so underestimates your power and your potency and the greater promise that humanity has for the future—for a future that will be unlike the past.

CHAPTER 8

PREPARING FOR THE GREATER COMMUNITY

As revealed to
Marshall Vian Summers
on April 15, 2011
in Boulder, Colorado

Humanity is preparing for the Greater Community. It does not know this yet, of course, but that is its stage of evolution, and everyone is involved. The fact that humanity is unprepared for the realities of contact with life in the universe is very apparent, but at a more unconscious level, people are anticipating this. And that is why it emerges in your movies, in your books, in human imagination. There is a seed of truth, an element of truth here.

There is a reason that people cannot speak of these things in public because it has been discouraged in the social discourse. That foreign craft are flying in your skies is an undeniable reality, and yet people do not want to think of it. And if they do think of it, they want to think of it in a positive way—that something wonderful is happening, that you have visitors, and they are here to help you and to guide you and to prepare you to meet the difficult challenges emerging in the world today.

You are preparing for the Greater Community. Unconsciously, perhaps foolishly and recklessly, you are preparing for the Greater Community. It is prepared for you. Races who are here in the world today are very well prepared for their mission here, a mission that few people in the world today comprehend and understand.

That is why the Revelation from God must reveal these things to you now in the clearest possible way so there can be no mistake, no tragic error of judgment, no misapprehension and no self-deception regarding the Intervention in the world today.

The wealth of the world is being spoiled and ruined, and the threat of this increasing has brought this Intervention here. It has also come because humanity has created an infrastructure that these races can utilize for themselves. You now have a worldwide community, worldwide communications, worldwide commerce and the beginnings of a worldwide government.

It is the great opportunity for the Intervention. They must act quickly before humanity destroys the wealth of the world, the wealth that the Intervention wants to have for itself. They also must act before humanity becomes more powerful, which would make Intervention more difficult to achieve.

It is a complex situation, and to understand it, you must have an education and preparation about the Greater Community of life itself—a reality that is unknown in the world. That is why the Revelation must speak of these things as well.

The religious traditions of the world were not given to prepare humanity for the Greater Community. Nor were they given to prepare humanity for a declining world—a world of diminishing resources and a world of escalating instability, a global community. The ancient teachings cannot prepare humanity for what is coming now, and who is here in your midst, and why they are here and the means they are using to achieve their goals of persuasion and dominance. These things must be revealed to an unwary and unprepared humanity.

You cannot stop the evolution of life. Even the evolution of civilization must proceed forward. You are going to have to face the Greater Community—ready or not, willing or not, prepared or not. If you are unwilling and unprepared and are not ready, then your position is extremely hazardous and the human family is in jeopardy.

These are greater matters that are not merely for people in privileged positions in government, or something for philosophers or theologians to consider. It is the concern and the focus of the citizens of the world. If they are unwilling to know and cannot respond, what can any government do?

That is why the Revelation is being brought to the citizens of the world, to you—to alert you, to prepare you, to strengthen you and to free you from illusions and misperceptions so that you may face the Greater Community clearly, honestly and objectively. For it is not a mystery, really. It is just a truth that is being concealed. It is being concealed by the governments of the world. It is being concealed by the Intervention itself. [Yet] it is part of nature.

You are facing competition from beyond the world. These forces are not here to eliminate humanity, but to corral humanity and to gain ascendancy in the world, for they cannot live in this environment. They need human assistance. It is a dangerous situation.

You will be afraid at first. You might even be in denial, thinking you do not want to deal with things of this nature. But this is the evolution of life. You must respond if you are to succeed. It is a great and difficult challenge, but humanity is able to face this challenge and to overcome it.

Forces in the world today are small. They cannot conquer the world by force, for that is not allowed in this region of space—something humanity knows nothing about.

To understand the Intervention, you must be educated about the Greater Community itself, and only God can educate you. For even a foreign race does not know the human heart and soul—even a beneficial foreign race, even those few races who are free in this region of space whom you could call "the Allies of Humanity," even they cannot really fully prepare you for this, for they do not know your heart and soul. They do not know your history. They are not your Source.

This is one of the great realities that must be faced at this time, a reality that will change your view and perspective of the world and make you realize that human conflict must cease and that humanity must prepare for the realities, the difficulties and the opportunities of the Greater Community.

God's Revelation has revealed how this can be done and what it means, and the realities and the spirituality of the Greater Community itself. This is part of your surviving in a radically changing world, for humanity is emerging out of isolation in the universe, and you will never have this isolation again.

Intervention is being attempted now, and even if it is thwarted, it will be attempted in the future. For the world is a prize, and humanity has not fully gained responsibility as the stewards of the world. You have not established a sustainable future, which opens the opportunities for Intervention.

Do not think that you are really important in the universe, that other races would come here to help you and be preoccupied with your wonderful characteristics. Do not fool yourself and congratulate yourself in this way. For you must have a sober approach, and you cannot lose heart and faith in humanity. The Intervention will try to strip you of self-confidence. That is one of their means of persuasion.

You must recognize that humanity has a destiny in the universe as a free and self-determined race, but to achieve this, you will have to learn Wisdom and Knowledge from the universe, which only God can really provide for you.

That is why the New Revelation is here, in part to prepare you for the Greater Community itself. The Revelation is also here to prepare you to live in a new world—a world of changing environments and political and social instability and upheaval.

The Revelation is here to teach you about spirituality at the level of Knowledge, the greater intelligence that God has placed within each person. The Revelation is here to bring you Knowledge and Wisdom from the universe so that you can prepare for life in the universe. And the Revelation is here to teach you of the Divine Presence, Plan and Will in the world, and to reveal the greater truth about these matters, and what it means for you and your life and destiny.

You have a great responsibility now to respond to the changing conditions of the world and to humanity's emergence into a Greater Community of life. You have a responsibility to learn of the Greater Community and to prepare for the Greater Community, and to become a person of the world and not merely a person of a small group, a tribe or a nation. For the whole world is being imperiled by the Intervention.

Do not let your national identity blind you to your greater responsibilities here. The preparation must be shared and must be considered. The veil of secrecy must be pulled aside. The veil of ridicule must be pulled aside. This must happen at the level of the citizens, for it cannot happen alone at the level of governments or leaders.

You are entering a greater panorama of life. You cannot be fooling around. You cannot be broadcasting your conflicts and your fantasies and your absurd interactions out into space. You must learn who is flying in your skies, who is taking your people against their will. This cannot be a deep dark secret now. It must come out into the open so that people can see it and understand it clearly. For, as We have said, it is not a mystery. It is a concealed truth, concealed by many forces.

The individual must see with clear eyes and not be dominated by the persuasions of governments or social conventions or social persuasions. If you are to be free, this must be the case. If you are to contribute to an emerging world, this must be the case. If you are to prepare for the Greater Community yourself, which is mostly an internal preparation, this must be the case.

As it is now, humanity will fall into the hands of the Intervention eventually unless great effort is made to resist the Intervention and to reveal its presence and purpose in the world. The Intervention has its human representatives, people it has taken against their will and turned to its persuasions. It is no different from what nations do to one another—to undermine each other, to overtake each other, to gain access to each other's resources and wealth. It is only happening on a more sophisticated and clandestine level now.

The secret must be revealed. It is clear. It is not ambiguous. All foreign races in the world today are part of the Intervention. The true Allies of Humanity will not intervene in human affairs, for if they had to intervene, they would have to control human understanding and perception, which as free races they will not do. And there are other reasons why they will not intervene, which you must learn of through the Revelation.

Knowingly or not, willingly or not, you are preparing for the Greater Community. This is one of the great needs of your time. If nations understood these things, human conflict would end. Human surveillance of the skies would become not just a matter for secret government agencies, but it would be a responsibility for citizens everywhere. The taking of people against their will would be revealed, and the Intervention would be exposed. It is relying upon human submission and human ignorance. If it is exposed, it must withdraw. This is the power that humanity could exert on its own behalf, which is not being exerted now.

The Greater Community education must begin. The time is late, the hour is late and the situation grows darker and more difficult with each passing day.

You were sent into the world to face these things. Regardless of your personal preoccupations, regardless of your preferences, regardless of your personal condition, this is the truth of your presence in the world. You were not sent into the world a hundred years ago when there was no Intervention here. You were not sent into the world fifty years ago, before the Intervention became truly manifest. This is your time and place. This is the world you have come to serve. Ignore this, and you will not find your true purpose and contribution in the world.

Some people have a connection with life in the universe, but everyone must face the Intervention. Everyone must begin their Greater Community education if humanity is to have a future as a free and self-determined race.

Competitors are in the world today functioning in a clandestine manner. How can you possibly understand this without the Revelation? You cannot prepare yourself for the Greater Community because you do not know what you are preparing yourself for. And human fantasy, speculation and projection regarding life in the universe have very little to do with the realities that you must face.

Do not shrink from this, for this is part of your calling. This is part of the required education of your time. This is what will motivate you to preserve the world, for your self-sufficiency in the universe is extremely important and is one of the necessary criteria to establish freedom and self-determination in the universe.

The Revelation is providing the preparation for the Greater Community, the only such preparation in the world today. The timing is critical. The need is tremendous, though it remains unseen and unrecognized by most people here.

Be courageous. Be determined. You must be courageous and determined to prepare for the Greater Community. You must be patient, for this is a greater education. It cannot be defined in a few sentences or simple definitions. You cannot be lazy and foolish in the face of such a great threshold.

God knows what is coming, and God must prepare humanity, who does not see and does not know. It is the challenge of facing the new world, a declining world, and the challenge of facing the Greater Community that will unite people and strengthen people and allow humanity to overcome its ancient conflicts and animosities.

You have a common need. It is so prevailing that it can overtake everything else. This is the gift of the great challenge you are facing—if this challenge can be comprehended, if the education about the Intervention and the Greater Community can be presented and shared.

Come to this and you will escape the petty matters of your life and your own suffering over little things. You will see the importance of your presence in the world and why you have been blessed and guided to receive the New Revelation.

Humanity has great promise in the universe, but for this promise to be realized, it must grow up. It cannot be adolescent. It cannot be foolish and self-indulgent in the face of greater things. Other forces are in your midst. You will have to contend with them now, and doing so will uplift humanity and give it greater strength and a greater determination for the future.

CHAPTER 9

PROTECTING THE WORLD

As revealed to
Marshall Vian Summers
on December 15, 2006
in Boulder, Colorado

It is apparent to many people that the environment is undergoing tremendous stress and in many places tremendous degradation. While a few people are very concerned, most people do not pay much attention to this, thinking that the environment is kind of an endless supplier of everything they need.

Many people today have lost sight of the utter dependence they have on their environment to provide them the bare essentials of life—food, water, shelter and clothing—and to make possible all of the conveniences and the benefits that they enjoy, to whatever extent these things are available to them.

But the environment has great power to change and alter the course of human destiny. Those who are aware of humanity's long history will understand this. The New Message from God emphasizes that the world's environment must be preserved and well cared for if humanity is to have a future. For if this is not done, humanity will decline, human conflict will escalate, and human deprivation and suffering will increase dramatically.

While this is apparent to a few people today, what many people do not realize is if humanity were to decline in this way, you would be extremely vulnerable to persuasion and influence from forces from the Greater Community, the Greater Community of intelligent life [in the universe] in which your world exists.

For there are many races today who are watching humanity—waiting for an opportunity to gain advantage here, waiting for an opportunity to gain access to this world's immense biological resources, waiting for an opportunity for humanity to be in a state of desperation where such influences will have tremendous impact.

This is the greatest threat to humanity's freedom and future. But it is a threat that very few people in the world today recognize or understand. For to be a free race within this Greater Community of intelligent life, you must be self-sufficient, you must be united and you must be extremely discreet.

Clearly, humanity can only benefit from one of these advantages, and that is that you are self-sufficient. You are hardly united. And you are hardly discreet.

Those races and groups who are watching the world from beyond, those races who seek to take advantage of a weak and divided humanity, can gain access to all your information. It is being broadcast into space. It is entirely available to the discreet observer.

You do not yet realize what a disadvantage this is, for you feel you are isolated in the universe and that no one can reach your shores. This is such a foolish assumption, of course. Such a ridiculous proposition. But this is what most people believe. This is what human science still advocates.

The human family has lived in isolation for so long that it assumes that isolation is a fact of life. But it is hardly a fact of life. If you could stand outside your world and observe the actions of intelligent races in the neighborhood in which your world exists, it would be quite apparent that humanity is in great peril.

Do not think that humanity has garnered much respect within this local environment. For indeed others see you destroying a world of immense value, a real gem in the universe, and so they seek to intervene. But they cannot do this militarily, for that is prevented in the area of space in which you live.

So they will seek more subtle and invasive means. Such means are already underway and are being taken by several competing groups who seek to have this world's splendid environment and resources for themselves.

Such groups do not seek to eradicate humanity but to wait until humanity is entirely dependent and compliant on whatever they may offer to you. That is why for the human family to lose its self-sufficiency is the greatest disadvantage that you could create for yourself. Even beyond the specter of human suffering, conflict and war, this would be your greatest disadvantage.

For the world could be overtaken without firing a shot. Humanity could fall under the persuasion of foreign powers far more easily than you realize. And this could be accomplished by humanity itself, with a minimum of foreign intervention and foreign persuasion.

This is why, you see, the environment is the most important thing— more important than personal wealth, more important than national military strength, more important than any country's national security. For the greater emphasis here is the world's security.

You have great barriers against one another. You have great walls of separation dividing the human family, making it weak, vulnerable and self-destructive. But you have no barriers against the Greater Community. And as the native peoples of this world, you are in a very vulnerable and precarious situation.

Human unity may be a long way away to achieve. Human discretion may be a long way away to achieve. But you must not lose your self-sufficiency. For if you do, then you will have to yield to whatever a foreign power will offer you. You will not be in a position to decline these offers. You will not be in a position to negotiate for your own best interests. You will receive whatever offerings are given. And you will allow these powers to establish themselves here, hoping and believing it is for your benefit.

This is the great peril that awaits humanity. It is a peril that any emerging race in the universe will have to face. For the first to reach the shores of this world will not be saints and environmentalists. The first to reach the shores of your world will be commercial interests, resource explorers, economic collectives, those who seek to take advantage of the native peoples—native peoples whom they do not respect or regard as their equals.

Indeed, at this moment humanity assumes its pre-eminence in the world. It feels it has a God-given right to be in this pre-eminent position within the world. But within this Greater Community, humanity is a weak, divided and self-obsessed race occupying and stewarding a planet of immense value and importance to others.

It is important, therefore, that you gain a Greater Community perspective on these things, for if you do, your understanding of the environment and your understanding of its importance to your future gain a whole new emphasis. It is an entirely practical emphasis.

For never think that you can go into space and just claim whatever resources that you have wasted here upon the Earth, for those resources are owned by others. Never assume that the universe is just a vast empty place awaiting human exploration and human exploitation. For you are not alone in the universe or even within your own world at this time.

The ignorance and the arrogance of such assumptions must be corrected, or humanity will make fatal mistakes that even God and God's Angels will not be able to offset.

That is why there is a New Message from God in the world because humanity is destroying its self-sufficiency, humanity is standing at the edge of space, and humanity is already experiencing forces that are intervening in its world, without its control and without its permission.

Though there are great perils facing humanity regarding the deterioration of your environments, climate change, decline of life-giving resources and so forth, the greatest peril—the peril that could end human sovereignty forever in this world—lurks in the background, awaiting the moment when humanity will bring itself to its knees through conflict, through deprivation, through war and through further decline of the world's environment.

God has given this world to humanity as a splendid place, as a paradise in a universe full of barren worlds. If you should ruin it, if you should exhaust its life-giving resources, if you should exhaust its biological diversity, then you will have to face the consequences, which will be far more terrible and far more longlasting than anything humanity as a whole has ever faced before.

Your real destiny is to emerge within this Greater Community of intelligent life as a free and sovereign race, but this requires that you meet the three requirements that are essential for any race to have such a privileged position in the universe. You must be self-sufficient. You must be united. And you must be extremely discreet.

Without this, humanity is but awaiting its own self-destruction. It is but awaiting the growing influence of foreign powers here, who seek to take control of the world and the world's peoples.

This is revealed through the New Message from God. This is part of what has brought the New Message from God into the world. For you live at a time of great urgency, not only for life at this moment but for the prospects for your future, which every day grow a little dimmer.

Some people believe the world is like a cornucopia that just provides endlessly. They just need the technology to gain more and more and more. But the world is a finite place with finite resources. If you exhaust it, you face the perils that such exhaustion will bring to you. This is a truth of life in the physical universe. You cannot escape it, whether you are a human being or whether you are a race living in another world, for the laws of nature hold true everywhere.

Therefore, the New Message from God emphasizes the importance of this self-sufficiency, the importance of human unity and the importance of learning to be discreet by understanding the nature of thought and power within the mental environment in which you live.

It is this mental environment, this environment of thought and influence, that humanity knows so little about and which you will need to understand with greater skill and potency in the future if you are to interact with other races successfully, other races who have gained skill in the mental environment.

The New Message from God emphasizes this tremendously, for God wills that humanity have a great future, a future greater than its past. But the prospect of gaining such a future is now in your hands, individually and collectively.

You are determining your future and the future of your children and of all people at this moment by what you think, by how you live, by what you promote and advocate and by how you identify yourself as a human being within this world.

If you believe you are only a member of one tribe or group or nation, you will not be able to support a greater movement towards human unity and cooperation. You will merely be one side competing with other sides—draining the world of its remaining resources, fighting over those resources, struggling over those resources.

The great hope for humanity lies in the mysterious power of Knowledge that the Creator has given to each person, that each person carries within themselves. It is this great spiritual power that goes unrecognized and unheard by the vast majority of people in the world today.

This power, then—should it be recognized, should it be understood, should it be received—will teach you how to live, will teach you how to relate to other people and to other nations and to other groups. It will teach you the importance of your thoughts and behavior. It will teach you everything you need to navigate the difficult times ahead and to navigate these times in such a way that you promote human freedom and unity in everything you do.

There is no human belief system or philosophy that could achieve this because they are human inventions. But this Knowledge is a God invention. It is God's Wisdom that has been placed within you.

But you must bring your mind and your thoughts in service to this power and to this greater intelligence if you are to receive its guidance, its protection and its benefits. That is why the New Message from God contains the teaching in The Way of Knowledge and shows how to take the Steps to Knowledge.

It begins then within the individual. For an individual guided by Knowledge is a powerful force—far more powerful than laws or legislation or social movements, though these things may emanate from the actions of such individuals. Then it becomes everyone's responsibility to make a difference—not only for themselves, not only to bring greater happiness and fulfillment into their lives, but to build a strong foundation for humanity's future.

For at every moment, you are living in the moment and building the future. And future generations will thank you or curse you depending on what you contribute today and the strength of your convictions to support human unity and freedom today.

This includes the sharing of resources. This includes extending wealth to people who need it. And also teaching how to live in such a way that people's environments and where they live can be sustained and can be productive.

With war and conflict, humanity will weaken and further its own decline. Should this be continued, there will be no winners. There will be no victorious nations or groups, for the world will decline. Then everyone will lose security. Then everyone will become weaker and more vulnerable to powers and influences from beyond the world who are determined to gain access and control here.

This is the great moment. This is the great time in which you live. This is a great calling for Knowledge within you to emerge in your awareness. This is a great calling for you to take the Steps to Knowledge, for you live at a great turning point.

It is a greater turning point than any of your ancestors ever faced. The future of humanity is being decided and will be decided in the next ten to fifteen years. That is how significant this time is.

Perhaps you yourself feel that your life is for a greater purpose, that you are here in the world to do something important—to make a difference, to contribute something of value here. If this is your experience, then you are responding to the great times in which you live and to the great needs of humanity. You are looking beyond your own personal needs and desires and responding to a greater power and a greater need in the world. This then is the evidence of Knowledge. It is very important that you respond to this.

The New Message from God is for this. It speaks to this awareness, to this need, to this inner understanding. It speaks to the need of the individual to discover the power and presence of Knowledge for themselves. And it speaks to the need of all humanity to build a foundation for the future, a future where you will realize you are not alone in the universe and that you must protect and safeguard this world.

To do this in whatever individual way you can means that you are fulfilling your greater purpose for coming into the world. This greater purpose is not based upon religious belief or ideology. It is based upon a fundamental responsibility, a responsibility of being true to the greater intelligence that the Creator has placed within you, which you are here to serve and to express.

You can be a person within a religion or a person without a religion and still respond to this great power within you and allow this great power to express itself and to contribute to the world through your thoughts and actions.

That is why the New Message from God is not just another belief system. It is a Message for all the peoples and all the religions of the world. It is a calling for human awareness, human unity and human responsibility. It holds true for all peoples, all nations and all faith traditions.

For this is the great time in which you live. This is the great turning point for which you have come. It is a great turning point that involves your life completely. It is a great turning point to which you are responsible.

No one from the outside, no one from the Greater Community, is going to come and rescue humanity. No technology is going to rescue humanity. No magic power from the Creator is going to come at the last hour and make all the difficulties go away.

God has already given you the answer. The answer is within Knowledge within you. This answer is not merely an idea or a prescription. It is a guiding power and influence. It is not bound by human religions or ideologies or philosophies because it is born of God. It is not a human creation. It is a God creation. And whether you believe in God or not, this power and this presence is available to you, and you need it so very greatly.

Recognize, then, that your environment is immensely important. Whatever you can do—whatever small action you can take, whatever is within the range of your personal skill, power and responsibility to enhance and to keep this environment healthy—is fundamental to your success.

You will feel within yourself that whatever you can do will generate a sense of satisfaction and a sense of value for you. This is entirely natural for you to feel this way, for this is why you have come into the world—to support human freedom and humanity's future and to care for the world that has been given to you to make this possible.

CHAPTER 10

THE IMPORTANCE OF THE GREATER COMMUNITY

As revealed to
Marshall Vian Summers
on December 11, 2009
in Phnom Penh, Cambodia

The importance of the Greater Community cannot be underestimated in the New Message because ultimately humanity is preparing for its future within this larger arena of intelligent life. But it is unprepared and has no way to prepare itself, facing now an Intervention from beyond the world by races who seek to take advantage of humanity's weakness and naiveté. This, more than anything else, has called the New Message from God into the world.

The need for this Revelation is so great, but people do not see the need. They do not yet recognize how vulnerable they are to the power of persuasion that is even now being cast over the world and which will only increase in the future times.

Humanity is in a very weak position, for it is depleting the world at a tremendous pace, and it is facing the Great Waves of change. It is facing environmental decline and the diminishing of its fundamental resources.

People do not see, and they do not understand the power of these times to alter the fate of humanity. They do not see the power of the Great Waves of change, and they do not see the power and the influence of the Greater Community. So their minds are elsewhere, concerned with other things. But God watches over the world and sends into the world what humanity needs, even if humanity cannot see this need itself.

The Greater Community is your destiny. But it is also your great hazard, for humanity is in the process of losing its self-sufficiency at an alarming rate, making it ever more vulnerable to foreign persuasion and intervention, making it ever more vulnerable to the introduction of foreign technology here as an inducement, as a great temptation.

There are very few people in the world today who understand humanity's real predicament here. For how could they? Not knowing what life is like beyond the borders of this world, not understanding the importance of this world to other races, not seeing that humanity is not highly regarded in this region of space? For you have not earned respect yet.

And so you are vulnerable, for you are wasting the world, a world that is valued by others. And this has sparked the Intervention that is now underway.

Even if this Intervention were to be thwarted, which is entirely possible and in your power to achieve, there will be future interventions. Thus, your position in life has changed. Your isolation is over. You must now contend with the Greater Community.

Humanity has allies abroad in your vicinity of space who understand your plight and who value the fact that humanity has kept religion and spirituality alive in the world and that the human family shows a greater promise—a promise that has been lost by so many advancing races in the universe.

Humanity is now vulnerable to persuasion and intervention and is weakening its position and the fabric of human unity. The Great Waves of change will only make this more tenuous and more dangerous in the face of the Greater Community.

Conquest is not allowed in this region of space, and it is not even considered because it would be too destructive to the world. Instead, this is an attempt to win humanity over—to promise humanity what it cannot provide for itself, to weaken the people's confidence in their governments and leaders, to weaken the human spirit, to lead people to acquiesce and to believe that the Intervention is here to help and to redeem a struggling humanity.

But it is all a deception. It is all a great lie. And yet people are believing in it. Every day people are being turned towards the Intervention. Having lost faith in humanity and in themselves, they will now seek the guidance and the promises of other powers in the universe, powers which are not human, and which do not value human freedom, and who do not comprehend the human spirit or human aspirations.

This is a great threshold in understanding. But essentially it is nature that you are facing now—competition in nature, competition for the world, a competition that will not be played out on battlefields but in the minds and the hearts of men and women.

Already humanity is moving into a position of extreme powerlessness in the universe. For once you lose your self-sufficiency, once you cannot provide for yourself, your position is weak and untenable and subject to all manner of persuasion and manipulation.

This is how the world will be given away, you see. A weak and disheartened humanity—weakened by conflict and war, weakened by deprivation, weakened by human corruption and ignorance—will turn to its new masters, unaware that it is giving over its own freedom and destiny to powers that it does not understand.

You may think this is impossible. "It cannot happen," you say. But it has happened countless times in the Greater Community as young emerging races have depleted their worlds so severely that they must now beg and plead for others to come and to intervene, opening the door for the worst kind of intrusions to take place.

People do not see this and are not responding correctly to the alien presence that is in the world today, which is only here for that purpose. That is why the Creator of all life has sent a New Message into the world to alert and to prepare humanity. This is why the Creator of all life has asked humanity's Allies to send wisdom to the world in a set of Briefings, Briefings from the Allies of Humanity—to prepare you for the Greater Community, and to warn you against premature contact and the reality of the Intervention that is taking place in the world today.

Surely you must know that intervention always leads to subjugation, unless the native peoples can resist. This has been the case throughout the history of your world and holds true in the Greater Community of life as well.

It is an unfortunate situation, but it does have the power to unite humanity in its own defense. It has the power to uplift you and to require you to become responsible and to cooperate with others for the preservation of the world.

Yet there is much deception regarding these things and much confusion as a result, and much hope and belief that anyone who would come to the world would be here to help humanity in its great difficulties.

But this is not the case, you see. That is why God has sent a New Message into the world to provide what humanity cannot provide for itself, to give you the power and the wisdom to see what is truly happening in the world today and what humanity's great challenges and opportunities really mean as you stand at the threshold of space.

There is only one Teaching in the world today that can prepare you for life in the universe. There is only one Teaching today that can tell you what is coming over the horizon of the world with real accuracy and prophecy. There is only one Teaching in the world that is a New Message from God and that is so comprehensive and complete that it should be considered in this way.

You have your backs to the universe. You must face this. Shocking though it might seem at first, you must face this. Surely, you must think and consider reasonably that eventually humanity would have to deal with the reality of life in the universe, not merely as a scientific hypothesis or some future possibility but as a dramatic reality in the world today.

But people are not aware of this, do not think of this and are not prepared for this—the greatest of all events in human history, the greatest danger of losing your freedom and sovereignty in this world and the greatest opportunity to forge human unity out of sheer necessity and purpose.

For nothing that you value in the world will be maintained if you should fall under foreign persuasion and domination. And no true ally of humanity would ever intervene in the world in this way nor try to wrestle control of the world from human leaders and human institutions. But that is exactly the purpose and the intent of the Intervention.

This is why you must now begin to realize you live in a Greater Community of intelligent life, a universe full of countless races of beings. But you know nothing of this environment, nor how to interact with it, nor how to tell friend from foe, nor how to discern deception when it occurs and how to protect yourself from manipulation and the great influences that will be cast over the minds and the hearts of people in the world. You do not know how to do these things, you see, and who in the world can teach you? Who in the world knows what is coming and knows how to prepare?

This requires a New Revelation from the Creator. For even friendly foreign races such as the Allies of Humanity do not know enough about the human heart and spirit, or the intricacies of human culture and society, or the full extent of human history to be able to guide you in this matter completely.

This will require a Revelation from God—a Revelation unlike any Revelation that has ever been sent into the world before, a Revelation for this time and for the times to come, a Revelation to prepare you for the Great Waves of change, a Revelation to prepare you for the realities of life in the universe, a Revelation that is here to teach you the power of spirituality at the level of Knowledge, a Teaching which has never been made available to the human family before, a Revelation that is to bring you Knowledge and Wisdom from the universe so that you can be prepared for this vast and complex arena of life, a Revelation that is here to teach you what human destiny really means and how it can be fulfilled in the highest manner possible.

You are living in a time of Revelation, and you are living in a time of Intervention. You are living at a time when the world's critical resources are being overspent and overused. You are living at a time when human civilization faces great danger from collapse from within and from intrusion from without, from the outside.

This is a time for humanity to end its adolescent behaviors, to end its ceaseless conflicts with itself and to prepare to engage with the Greater Community. This will take the genius of humanity and all of its talents and all of its true leaders and experts to achieve. But none of them will know what to do. None of them will see the importance without this Revelation.

A Messenger has brought this into the world. He has brought Wisdom from the Greater Community. He has brought the Teaching in Greater Community Spirituality. He has brought the preparation in The Way of Knowledge so that people can take the Steps to Knowledge themselves. He has brought the warning about the Great Waves of change. And he has brought the warning about the Greater Community.

This has everything to do with who you are and why you are in the world at this time. For you did not come here by accident. You did not come here to live in a peaceful world, in a quiescent world, in a world that would not face the Great Waves of change. You have come at this time because of the Greater Community and because of the great travail humanity is facing, living in a declining world.

Perhaps you do not think of this yet or conceive of your life in this context, but from a higher vantage point, from a position of clarity and discernment, this is so obviously the case. But what is obvious is lost upon those who cannot see. It is never considered by those whose minds are caught up in other things.

This is why the Revelation must occur, and this is why it must come with the Power of the Creator. For the Creator is not merely sending ideas into the world. The Creator is sending Power into the world—the Power to redeem the individual, to bring clarity and purpose to the individual, so that their greater gifts may come forward in service to a world in need.

You are facing a turbulent and difficult future in the world, a world that will be under great challenge and stress. It all really has to do with the Greater Community, but you cannot see this yet, perhaps, for your mind is still focused on the human family and its problems alone. It is because humanity is declining that the Greater Community is in the world, seeing its great opportunity to gain control of this world through the power of persuasion and inducement.

You do not see that this is part of humanity's evolution. Like many races in the history of the universe, you have to face intervention. But only the Revelation from God will tell you what this means and what you will need to do to be successful here.

There are many teachings in the world today that address many different problems and different needs, but there is no greater problem or greater need for the human family than to prepare for the Great Waves of change and for the Greater Community. Because people do not know this, do not see this and do not comprehend this, that is really the core problem, you see.

If your nations and their leaders knew the peril facing humanity, war would end tomorrow. There would be no talk of conflict. There would be talk of preparation; there would be talk of contribution; there would be talk of cooperation, for the world is being endangered.

These are the great times before you now. This is why you must learn of the Greater Community, to see it as it really is and not as people want it to be, not filled with the projections of hope and fear. You must see the real Greater Community, and only God's New Revelation can show this to you.

You cannot wait a century for science to discover the essential things. You cannot take generations to be able to reach beyond the limits of this solar system. For the Intervention is underway, and it is gaining strength every day.

Humanity now finds itself in the midst of a larger set of circumstances, facing greater challenges and so forth. Do not shrink from this, for this is why you have come. This is the great turning point for humanity. But what humanity will choose and the degree of awareness that humanity has will make all the difference in which outcome occurs.

Is this the end of human civilization and human freedom, or is it the beginning of a new chapter in humanity's long evolution in the world? The answer is yet uncertain because the decisions have not yet been really made.

Therefore, life is challenging you, but it is also giving you strength. It is calling you out of the shadows, out of an empty pursuit for fulfillment—a pursuit that can only lead to confusion and despair. It is calling you to protect the world, to protect the human family. It is calling you to learn about the Greater Community and to receive the gifts of those in space who are aware of you and your plight, and who are seeking to help you by sharing their wisdom with you.

They will not come to the world or seek to influence human thinking or manipulate human behavior. But they do not want to see you fall under the persuasion of foreign powers. They know you have the power to resist—the power to resist intervention, the power to resist subjugation, the power to resist deception, deception that is practiced so often in the universe against the weak and unsuspecting.

It is time for your education about life to enter a greater and more mature phase. Here things must be revealed to you that you could not find before. Here you must be shown things that you could not see before and that you would probably never find upon your own.

Here a new vision and wisdom must be given to the human family. Here the individual must become strong and guided by the power of Knowledge within themselves. Here humanity must unite to protect the world, to renew the world and to establish a foundation that can sustain you into the future.

What God knows to be true and what humanity wants are not the same, and that is the great challenge before you. But what God knows, you cannot yet see. So it is being revealed to you now in the clearest possible terms. It is being revealed in such a way to call forth from you your greater strength and determination. It is to show you the power of Knowledge within yourself that will protect you from deception and that will give you the courage to see what must be done and the strength to carry it out.

We send Our blessings to you and Our encouragement. May all that has been given to humanity now be utilized to the fullest in the face of a Greater Darkness in the world, in the face of the great turning point for humanity.

CHAPTER 11

THE NEW REVELATION

As revealed to
Marshall Vian Summers
on August 24, 2008
in Boulder, Colorado

God has sent a New Message into the world. It is a Revelation for this time and the times to come. For humanity is entering a very dangerous period, a period where the Great Waves of change will be coming to the world: environmental degradation; the depletion of your resources; the changing of your climate; violent weather; economic instability and the growing risk of competition, conflict and war. It is a time when humanity will be facing the reality of an Intervention from races from beyond the world who are here to take advantage of a weak and divided humanity.

It will be a time of unprecedented instability. There will be great human need and suffering. It is a dangerous time for the human family, for the temptation to go to war to lay claim to the remaining resources will be very strong. And the needs of people in every country, even the wealthy nations, will be profound.

What will humanity do in the face of these two great challenges? That will be a deciding question, not only for governments and leaders, but for citizens as well—for everyone, for you. It will be a point of decision, and the decision will determine the outcome to a very great degree.

If humanity chooses the path that it has chosen in the past, to fight and to struggle, then human civilization will decline. And those foreign powers who are in the world today will gain pre-eminence here. Their offerings of technology you will not be able to deny.

It will be a sad ending to humanity's long and great development and evolution, to end in servitude to a foreign power, to capitulate. It will be a sad ending to what could have been a far greater story. But this outcome has not yet been chosen, and the way is clear for the human family to choose another path, a path of resolution and a path of cooperation in the face of great change and threats.

Only something catastrophic will unite humanity. And now you have the threat of catastrophe from within your world and from beyond your world. This is how races of people grow and evolve—out of necessity. But in order for humanity to choose the path of resolution and commitment and cooperation, it must have a greater vision, it must have a greater strength, and only a Revelation from God can provide this.

Humanity is not yet strong enough with Knowledge, the deeper wisdom that God has placed within the human family, to overcome its divisive tendencies, to overcome unforgiveness, to overcome grievances, to overcome ambition and to resist the temptation to fight and to struggle for what you need.

Humanity must grow up. It is still a primitive race in so many ways. It is still given to competition, conflict and war. It is not yet really seeing the necessity of a united human family—united out of necessity, united to face a declining world and united to face the competitive environment of the Greater Community of life in the universe. What will prevail, strength or weakness, within the minds and the hearts of people and in the policies of nations?

God's New Revelation is needed now, for humanity cannot prepare accordingly and adequately for a future that will be unlike the past without this Revelation. It is the power of Knowledge within the individual, and within many individuals, that will override your more primitive and self-destructive tendencies.

Optimism and high idealism will not be enough now. You must choose a pathway within yourself as an individual. If you yourself cannot rise above anger and anguish and resentment and the projection of blame upon others, then do not expect your leaders to do any better.

The Revelation is here to reveal humanity's inner strength and the requirements in your outer life that will call upon this strength and require it. The Revelation will show you what is coming in the Great Waves of change. It will reveal the Intervention that is occurring in the world today by those races from the universe who seek to gain advantage here. It will reveal your deeper nature, the power and the presence of Knowledge within yourself, which is the source of your strength and integrity, a power that is beyond deception and corruption. The great events of your time, which humanity cannot yet see clearly, which humanity does not have the courage yet to see clearly, are being revealed in a New Message from God.

The human family will face great travail in the future, much of it the result of its own abuse and overuse of the world and its unwise use of the world's resources. But this also represents an evolutionary step. For as your technology grows, so does the demand upon your world grow with it. As your population increases, you are pushing the world beyond its limits, its carrying capacity. What will you do with this?

There is a maturation process here because all nations and worlds that advance in the Greater Community have to face these kinds of thresholds. That is why every advanced nation in the universe that has been able to survive the rigors of competition with other nations and the difficulties in physical life has had to control their populations, has had to control the consumption of resources in order to become stable because you cannot simply go and consume more from the universe. Many people think the universe is just a big empty place like a wilderness and you will go out and get whatever you need there, but this is not the case. Once you venture beyond this solar system, you are entering the territories that are controlled by others. And they are far more powerful then you are.

You must face this fundamental problem in life of establishing stability and security. That represents the next great threshold for human development. It will not be growth and expansion, for you are reaching the limits of growth and expansion. Instead, it will be stability and security.

This is the difference between adolescence and adulthood. In adolescence, your life is expanding. It is opening up. It is reaching out. But in adulthood, you have to find stability and security if you are to be mature.

It is not about having more. It is not about consuming endlessly more. It is about finding a stable reality within the limits of your environment. This represents a fundamental shift in human awareness, a fundamental change in how you run your nations and your economies—a change of heart, a deeper recognition.

The universe is not yours for the taking, and should you try to take it, you will find yourself opposed by hundreds of nations.

The Revelation must come from God, but it must also take place within you, a kind of deeper reckoning and evaluation, a recognition that you are here to be of service to the world. You are not here to be a locust upon the field, devouring everything in sight. You are here to be a contributor to the world. And the gifts are within you, held within Knowledge deep within you, beyond the realm and reach of your intellect.

God's New Revelation will teach you how to find your gifts. But it will teach you this within the context of what is really occurring within the world so that your gifts can be realized and called out of you by the reality of the world in which you live. You cannot call these gifts out of yourself. They must be called out of you from the outside. If you are here to serve a world in transition, you must face a world in transition to have your contribution called out of you.

The need for this recognition is profound. Humanity is going blind into the future. You have your backs to the universe. You are not paying attention. Humanity is like on a train that cannot stop. Its throttle is stuck. It is driving headlong into calamity.

What will restrain this? What will mitigate this? What will help prepare humanity for the difficult times ahead? Surely, humanity is clever, but the wisdom required to really meet this greater set of needs is beyond your skill and scope.

That is why there must be a New Revelation, for you are entering a new period in your evolution. You are passing through a greater threshold that your ancestors never had to face. You are emerging into a much different environment with requirements and limitations that pose extraordinary problems for humanity as a whole, and yet [hold] extraordinary gifts as well. For it is only under these conditions that humanity will ever have the chance to overcome its ceaseless conflicts and its bitter dissensions within itself to establish a greater foundation of unity and cooperation.

Humanity is emerging into a Greater Community of intelligent life in the universe. If you are to remain free and self-determined, you cannot be a world of warring tribes, of divided nations. You will have to create a greater foundation of unity. You will have to have a united voice in speaking to the Greater Community and in resisting its interventions and competition from beyond.

The fact that this all seems to be too much for most people tells you that humanity is not yet strong enough or competent enough to deal with a greater set of issues and to face the reality of the Greater Community, or even to meet its overwhelming and growing problems here at home.

But God has placed within you the power of integrity, the power of commitment, the power of wisdom and compassion. This will give you the power and the clarity and the conviction to face an uncertain future with determination, with clarity and with courage.

Your emotions cannot provide this for you. Your ideals cannot provide this for you. Your theories and philosophies cannot provide this for you. This strength must come from the well of Knowledge within yourself. It is within you now, but you are not living according to its power and its presence. That is why taking the steps to this deeper Knowledge is so essential and is so much a part of preparing for the future.

God has sent many great teachings into the world to civilize humanity, to give it a higher ethical standard, to teach different paths of redemption for different people at different times. But now you are facing a set of circumstances that are radically different. You are facing a world in decline, and you are facing competition from the Greater Community itself.

That is why a New Revelation must be given to the world. This Revelation will resonate with all that is true within the world's religious traditions, for at the core of them all is the Knowledge and the reality of your spiritual identity, and the truth that you were sent into the world for a greater purpose.

God has initiated all the world's great religions, but they have all been changed and altered by people and culture, and now they appear to be in competition and conflict with one another. What seems different between them is what is emphasized. People have different heroes, different teachers, different interpretations, and these are vehemently expressed, and sometimes violently expressed. But the true nature of the world's religions is fundamentally that you are born of God, that there is one God, and that you are here in the world to be of service to a struggling humanity.

This is exactly what God's New Message emphasizes. But God's New Message also teaches you to function within a declining world and teaches you how to prepare for a Greater Community of intelligent life, which humanity has never had to face before. It is not the same as an ancient race being visited from races from the Greater Community. Now you are facing the reality of the Greater Community itself—a difficult and challenging reality, a reality where freedom is rare, a reality that is not governed by human values and human temperament, a very competitive reality where the powers of persuasion are strong.

You have not yet adapted to this greater reality. You do not even know what it is, and yet it is upon you. You are now facing it because there is Intervention in the world by races who are here to exploit human weakness and to gain advantage to the great biological resources of the world.

You are being thrust into this larger arena of life, but you are unprepared and unaware. You cannot be foolish here. You cannot fantasize here and have any hope of being effective or of protecting human freedom within this larger arena of life.

You must become united. You must be powerful. You must be clear. Only a New Revelation from God can teach this to you and give this to you and reveal what you could not know otherwise in order to prepare you for your destiny in the Greater Community.

The fact that most people will not respond is not the issue. Whenever God has sent a New Revelation into the world, most people would not or could not respond. The response came to a few, and it was their response and responsibility that enabled God's Revelation to come into the world, and to be of benefit within the world, and to be sustained within the world over time.

Religion has suffered many tragic errors, but at its core it is redeeming and powerful, for it evokes a greater set of ethics and a greater strength and compassion within the human heart, which separates you from the beasts of the field, which separates you from your more primitive ancestors. It is this inner strength that humanity will need or you will not have the courage or the commitment or the clarity to face a very uncertain future with immense and unanticipated challenges.

God knows what is coming for the world. God knows that humanity cannot prepare without a New Revelation. And so a New Revelation is being sent into the world for the protection and the advancement of humanity.

If you are a practitioner of a religious tradition, do not be threatened by this. It is here to resonate with the essence and the core of your religious faith. It is a Message from the same God that has provided you your pathway in life. It is a New Testament. It is here to enliven your religion and to expand it, to make its realm of application greater. It is here to prepare you. It is providential.

If you deny this, you deny the Source of your religious faith and tradition. If you take issue against God's New Revelation, then you are in conflict with your own tradition and its Source. If you dispute that a New Revelation could come into the world, then you are being arrogant, assuming that you know God's Will and that God's Will will conform to your beliefs and expectations. Do not be presumptuous and say that the last prophet has spoken, for that is to assume God's Will.

Do not make this assumption, for there is a New Revelation in the world. It is here to meet an unprecedented set of circumstances and needs. It is here to prepare you for a future that will be unlike the past. It is here to rescue humanity from its own self-destruction. And it is here to protect humanity from exploitation from the Greater Community and to prepare humanity for the reality of this Greater Community, which represents your future and your destiny.

Do not condemn the man chosen to receive and bring this New Message into the world. He is a humble man. He has no position, and yet he is imbued with a New Message from God. You may challenge him and question him, but do not condemn him until you have really examined the New Message and have taken it into your heart, or you will make the same error as those made who condemned God's previous Messengers.

Do not think that this man is functioning without the complete support of Jesus and Muhammad and the Buddha and all the great Teachers and Emissaries that have been sent into the world over time, for he is carrying on their tradition. He is not a savior. He is a Messenger. He does not require devotion or worship because he is only a man. But he *is* the Messenger. And he will have to face all the problems of criticism and condemnation and ridicule and ambivalence that all the Messengers have all had to face in their own eras and times.

It is the same problem that people face today. They are governed by beliefs and ideas and their own social conditioning. They do not see clearly with the power of Knowledge that God has placed within them, for they have not yet gained access to this greater strength. And that is the fundamental problem that humanity faces in all of its dilemmas and conflicts and tragedies.

With Knowledge, these conflicts would not arise or would be resolved quickly. Without Knowledge, small problems become big problems. Big problems become endemic and ingrained in cultures. Divisions are long standing, and wars continue to erupt.

It is like the planet you live on. It seems quiescent and stable on the surface, but underneath there is molten rock. It is violent. It is intense.

A life without Knowledge is like that. It may seem placid and stable on the outside, but underneath it is roiling. It is turbulent. It is violent. And this violence will erupt. It will erupt in people's individual lives. It erupts within the human family in the form of conflict and war and catastrophe.

It is because humanity is not yet connected to Knowledge and the wisdom that Knowledge would provide that it is in contention with itself ceaselessly and that these contentions and conflicts seem to be beyond resolution. They perpetuate themselves. Groups of people have been at odds with each other for centuries, projecting blame upon each other, distrusting each other.

With Knowledge, this would not be the case. For Knowledge would override these tendencies and would give you a greater vision and equanimity, and a greater recognition of one another. To face the Greater Community, Americans and Chinese and Russians and Iranians and the peoples from all the nations of the world will have to cooperate if humanity is to survive and to avoid intervention. In facing the Great Waves of change, nations will have to cooperate with each other to provide resources to each other, or the human family will begin to fail.

The rich will have to take care of the poor, or civilization will fall apart. It is because you are facing a world in decline and you are facing competition from beyond the world that this is the case.

It is not like the past, for you are exceeding now the world's carrying capacity. There will be shortages of food, lack of energy resources. Many places will become uninhabitable in the future because of changing climate and the loss of water. It is not like the past where the rich can content themselves with their own personal pursuits, hobbies and obsessions and the rest of society struggles and declines. You cannot function like that in the future.

God knows this. Humanity does not see it yet. God knows that you will have to unite to survive in the future. Humanity does not see this yet. God knows that you will have to become strong and resist intervention from beyond the world, but humanity does not see this yet. God knows that you have gone too far in your use of resources and have used them recklessly, destroying your natural inheritance here in the world, but humanity does not see this yet.

God knows that you cannot afford war and conflict for any reason. Humanity does not see this yet. God knows that nations cannot try to overcome each other and dominate each other if humanity is to have the stability and the unity necessary to survive into the future. But humanity does not see this yet. God knows that humanity will not be able to find the resources it depletes here on earth in searching space. But humanity does not see this yet. God knows that if humanity accepts technology from foreign races, that it will become dependent upon those races and will lose power and self-determination to those races. But humanity does not see this yet.

This is why there is a greater Revelation in the world. It will go unnoticed. It will be rejected, avoided and denied, but that is what has happened to all God's Revelations. In that sense, nothing has really changed.

But your environment has changed. Your circumstances are changing beyond your recognition. You are facing competition from beyond the world for who will be pre-eminent in this world and who will govern its resources and its environment.

It is not about your hopes and your fears now, for this is a time when you must see clearly. And you must have a New Revelation to see clearly because without this, humanity will not see clearly. It will believe in its fantasies. It will believe in its predictions. It will follow its premonitions. It will be subject to its conflicts and its grievances.

You cannot function like this in the future if human civilization is going to survive and if human freedom is going to survive and to evolve. God knows this. But humanity is not yet aware of it.

This is the problem. But through the Revelation, an answer is being given. But if you cannot see the problem, you will not see the answer.

If you cannot recognize the deeper need for you to know who you are and why you are in the world and what you are here to accomplish, your life will just be a mass of confusion—a puzzle that you cannot put together, full of contradictions, full of uncertainties, full of self-recrimination, full of errors. That is why there is a New Revelation.

The world is like your life in that regard. It is a mass of confusion, full of beliefs, full of fantasies, full of fear, full of error and tragedy, lost opportunities, failed attempts—all consuming humanity's time, energy and resources when all along God has given you a more powerful Presence within yourself to guide you, to lead you and to help you escape seduction and deception. You will need this power now. It will not simply be the providence of the enlightened or inspired few. It will have to be something that runs deeper within the entire human family.

Human wisdom, which is imbedded within you, which God has created for you, will now have to become relied upon and utilized. You must begin to listen to those who are wise in your nations, those who are pragmatic, those who realize that ideology is blind and that belief alone is blind.

For now God has given you a greater power, a greater vision and a greater skill. And it is this that humanity must foster, nourish and encourage in its young people, in its citizens, if it is to become and remain a free nation in a universe where freedom is rare. God knows this. But people do not recognize it yet.

Accept your limitations here with humility and with relief, for you cannot govern your life based upon ideas alone. You need a greater power and a greater sense of justice and compassion that is not based upon ideology or political views or religious beliefs or human greed, human fear, human aggravation.

God has given you an ethical foundation that is held with Knowledge within yourself. You know that thievery is wrong. You know that murder is wrong. You know that bearing false witness is wrong. The commandments have been given. What is the problem?

The problem is that humanity does not have the strength, the courage and the commitment to follow them. This courage and commitment does not come from the intellect or from your emotions or from your beliefs. It comes from the power of Knowledge within you.

That is why the Revelation that God is providing humanity now addresses the reality of your spiritual life at the level of Knowledge. It is only here that you will find not only the vision of the truth, but the strength and the power and the commitment to follow it.

When you finally realize that you cannot manage your life, that you cannot solve the problems of the world, that you do not know how to face the Great Waves of change and that you have no idea how to prepare for a Greater Community of intelligent life, then you will turn to Knowledge within yourself. This is where God will speak to you, and this is where you will find the well of strength, integrity and courage that you will need to face the great difficulties and uncertainties of this time.

Only God can give this to you, and God has given this to you already. You may argue against it, you may contend against it, you may disavow it, but you cannot change it. There is your mind and there is Knowledge, which is a deeper mind within you. Knowledge will not follow your mind, your intellect, but your intellect must follow Knowledge if it is to be truly effective and constructive. God knows this is true. But humanity has not yet realized this.

That is why there is a New Revelation in the world. It is unlike any Revelation that has ever been sent to the world before. It will build upon all the great Revelations that have been sent to this world, but it will reveal things that humanity has never seen or known before. For this is required now to prepare humanity for its next great stage of evolution, and to prepare humanity to face the great and unprecedented challenges of this time.

IMPORTANT TERMS

―――――

$\mathscr{T}$he New Message from God reveals that our world stands at the greatest threshold in the history and evolution of humanity. At this threshold, a New Message from God has come. It reveals the great change that is coming to the world and our destiny within the Greater Community of life beyond our world, for which we are unaware and unprepared.

Here the Revelation redefines certain familiar terms, but within a greater context, and introduces other terms that are new to the human family. It is important to understand these terms when reading the texts of the New Message.

―――――

GOD is revealed in the New Message as the Source and Creator of all life and of countless races in the universe. Here the greater reality of God is unveiled in the expanded context of all life in this world and all life in the universe. This greater context redefines the meaning of our understanding of God and of God's Power and Presence in our lives. The New Message states that to understand what God is doing in our world, we must understand what God is doing in the entire universe. This understanding is now being revealed for the first time through a New Message from God. In the New Message, God is not a personage or a singular awareness, but instead a pervasive force and reality that permeates all life, existing beyond the limited boundaries of all theology and religious understanding. God speaks to the deepest part of each person through the power of Knowledge that lives within them.

THE SEPARATION is the ongoing state and condition of being separate from God. The Separation began when part of Creation willed to have the freedom to be apart from God, to live in a state of Separation. As a result, God created our evolving world and the expanding universe as a place for the separated to live in countless forms and places. Before the Separation, all life was in a timeless state of pure union. It is to this original state of union with God that all those living in Separation are ultimately called to return—through service, contribution and the discovery of Knowledge. It is God's mission in our world and throughout the universe to reclaim the separated through Knowledge, which is the part of each individual still connected to God.

KNOWLEDGE is the deeper spiritual mind and intelligence within each person, waiting to be discovered. Knowledge represents the eternal part of us that has never left God. The New Message speaks of Knowledge as the great hope for humanity, an inner power at the heart of each person that God's New Message is here to reveal and to call forth. Knowledge exists beyond the intellect. It alone has the power to guide each of us to our higher purpose and destined relationships in life.

THE NEW MESSAGE FROM GOD is an original Revelation and communication from God to the people of the world, both for our time and the times to come. The New Message is a gift from the Creator of all life to people of all nations and religions and represents the next great expression of God's Will and Plan for the human family. The New Message is over 9000 pages in length and is the largest Revelation ever given to the world, given now to a literate world of global communication and growing global awareness. The New Message is not an offshoot or reformation of any past tradition. It is a New Message from God for humanity, which now faces great instability and upheaval in the world and the great threshold of emerging into a Greater Community of intelligent life in the universe.

IMPORTANT TERMS

THE MESSENGER is the one chosen, prepared and sent into the world by the Angelic Assembly to receive the New Message from God. The Messenger for this time is Marshall Vian Summers. He is a humble man with no position in the world who has undergone a long and difficult preparation to be able to fulfill such an important role and mission in life. He is charged with a great burden, blessing and responsibility to receive God's pure Revelation and to protect and present it in the world. He is the first of God's Messengers to reveal the reality of a Greater Community of intelligent life in the universe. The Messenger has been engaged in a process of Revelation for over 30 years. He is alive in the world today.

THE PRESENCE can refer to either the presence of Knowledge within the individual, the Presence of the Angelic Assembly or ultimately the Presence of God. The Presence of these three realities offers a life-changing experience of grace and relationship that can be found by following the mystery in life and by studying and practicing either one of God's past Revelations, or God's New Revelation for the world. The New Revelation offers a modern pathway to experiencing the power of this Presence in your life.

STEPS TO KNOWLEDGE is an ancient book of spiritual practice now being given by God to the world for the first time. In taking this mysterious journey, each person is led to the discovery of the power of Knowledge and the experience of profound inner knowing, which can lead them to their higher purpose and calling in life.

THE ALLIES OF HUMANITY refers to those in the universe who are allied with God's Work in the Greater Community and support humanity's emergence as a free and self-determined race. The Allies of Humanity have sent a small group of individuals from several different worlds to gather in the vicinity of Earth in order to observe, report and advise us on the activities of the alien Intervention that is

149

taking place in the world today. This group of observers has provided to the world multiple sets of Briefings on the Intervention which can be read at www.alliesofhumanity.org.

THE COLLECTIVES are complex, hierarchical organizations composed of different alien races bound together for common economic goals. The collectives are largely responsible for the Intervention that is occurring in our world. There is more than one Collective present in the world today.

THE GREATER COMMUNITY is the larger universe of intelligent life in which our world has always existed. This Greater Community encompasses all worlds in the universe where sentient life exists, in all states of evolution and development. The New Message reveals that humanity is in an early and adolescent phase of its development and that the time has now come for humanity to prepare to emerge into the Greater Community. It is here, standing at the threshold of space, that humanity discovers that it is not alone in the universe, or even within its own world.

THE GREATER COMMUNITY WAY OF KNOWLEDGE represents God's work in the universe, which is to reclaim the separated in all worlds through the power of Knowledge that is inherent in all intelligent life. To understand what God is doing in our world, we must begin to understand what God is doing in the entire universe. For the first time in history, The Greater Community Way of Knowledge is being presented to the world through a New Message from God. The New Message opens the portal to this timeless work of God underway throughout the Greater Community of life in the universe. We who stand at the threshold of emerging into this Greater Community must have access to this greater reality and this pathway of redemption in order to understand our future and destiny as a race.

THE ANGELIC ASSEMBLY is the great Angelic Presence that watches over the world. This Assembly is part of the hierarchy of service and relationship established by God to oversee the redemption and return of all separate life in the universe. Every world where sentient life exists is watched over by an Angelic Assembly. The Assembly overseeing our world has translated the Will of God for our time into human language and understanding, which is now revealed through the New Message from God. The term Angelic Assembly is synonymous with the terms Angelic Presence and Angelic Host.

THE VOICE OF REVELATION is the united voice of the Angelic Assembly, delivering God's Message through a Messenger sent into the world for this task. Here the Assembly speaks as one Voice, the many speaking as one. For the very first time in history, you are able to hear the actual Voice of Revelation speaking through God's Messenger. It is this Voice that has spoken to all God's Messengers in the past. The Word and the Sound of the Voice of Revelation are in the world anew.

THE INTERVENTION refers to a silent invasion into our world by multiple alien races and organizations for the purpose of gaining access to the resources, people and strategic position of the Earth. In order to advance their agenda for control and influence, the Intervention is engaged in four fundamental activities: influencing and controlling individuals in positions of power and authority, the creation of hidden establishments from which the Intervention can influence human populations in the mental environment, the manipulation of religious values and impulses in order to gain human allegiance and finally an interbreeding program designed to create a hybrid race and a new leadership allegiant to the Intervention itself.

THE GREATER DARKNESS refers to the Alien Intervention underway by certain races from the Greater Community who are here to take advantage of a weak and divided humanity. This Intervention is occurring at a time when the human family is entering a period of increasing breakdown and disorder in the face of the Great Waves of change. The Intervention presents itself as a benign and redeeming force, while in reality its ultimate goal is to undermine human freedom and self-determination and take control of the world and its resources. The New Message reveals that the Intervention seeks to secretly establish its influence here in the minds and hearts of people at a time of growing confusion, conflict and vulnerability. As the native peoples of this world, we are called upon to oppose this Intervention and to alert and educate others, thus uniting the human family in a great common purpose, and preparing our world for the challenges and opportunities of life in the Greater Community.

THE GREAT WAVES OF CHANGE are a set of powerful environmental, economic and social forces now converging upon the world. The Great Waves are the result of humanity's misuse and overuse of the world, its resources and its environment. The Great Waves have the power to drastically alter the face of the world—producing economic instability, runaway climate change, violent weather and the loss of arable land and freshwater resources, threatening to produce a world condition of great difficulty and human suffering. The Great Waves are not an end times or apocalyptic event, but instead a period of transition to a new world condition. The New Message reveals what is coming for the world and the greater preparation that must be undertaken by enough people. It is calling for human unity and cooperation born now out of sheer necessity for the preservation and protection of human civilization.

THE MESSENGER

Marshall Vian Summers is the Messenger for the New Message from God. For over three decades he has been the recipient of a vast New Revelation, given to prepare humanity for the great environmental, social and economic changes that are coming to the world and for humanity's emergence into a universe of intelligent life.

In 1982, at the age of 33, Marshall Vian Summers had a direct encounter with the Angelic Presence who had been guiding and preparing him for his future role and calling. This encounter forever altered the course of his life and initiated him into a deeper relationship with the Angelic Assembly, requiring that he surrender his life to God. This began the long, mysterious process of receiving God's New Message for humanity.

Following this mysterious initiation, he received the first revelations of the New Message from God. Over the decades since, a vast Revelation for humanity has unfolded, at times slowly and at times in great torrents. During these long years, he had to proceed with the support of only a few individuals, not knowing what this growing Revelation would mean and where it would ultimately lead.

The Messenger has walked a long and difficult road to receive and present the largest Revelation ever given to the human family. Still today the Voice of Revelation continues to flow through him as he faces the great challenge of bringing God's New Revelation to a troubled and conflicted world.

Read and hear the Story of the Messenger:
www.newmessage.org/story

Hear and watch the world teachings of the Messenger:
www.newmessage.org/messenger

The Voice of Revelation

For the first time in history, you can hear the Voice of Revelation, such a Voice as spoke to the prophets and Messengers of the past and is now speaking again through a new Messenger who is in the world today.

The Voice of Revelation is not the voice of one individual, but that of the entire Angelic Assembly speaking together, all as one. Here God communicates beyond words to the Angelic Assembly, who then translate God's Message into human words and language that we can comprehend.

The revelations of this book were originally spoken in this manner by the Voice of Revelation through the Messenger Marshall Vian Summers. This process of Divine Revelation has occurred since 1982. The Revelation continues to this day.

The original audio recordings of the Voice of Revelation
are made available to all people.
To hear the Voice, which is the source of
the text contained in this book and throughout
the New Message, please visit:
www.newmessage.org/experience

To learn more about the Voice of Revelation, what it is
and how it speaks through the Messenger, visit:
www.newmessage.org/voiceofrevelation

About The Society for the New Message from God

Founded in 1992 by Marshall Vian Summers, The Society for the New Message from God is an independent religious 501(c)(3) non-profit organization that is primarily supported by readers and students of the New Message, receiving no sponsorship or revenue from any government or religious organization.

The Society's mission is to bring the New Message from God to people everywhere so that humanity can find its common ground, preserve the Earth, protect human freedom and advance human civilization as we stand at the threshold of space.

Marshall Vian Summers and The Society have been given the immense responsibility of bringing the New Message into the world. The members of The Society are a small group of dedicated individuals who have committed their lives to fulfill this mission. For them, it is a burden and a great blessing to give themselves wholeheartedly in this great service to humanity.

The Society for the New Message

Contact us:

P.O. Box 1724 Boulder, CO 80306-1724
(303) 938-8401 (800) 938-3891
011 303 938 84 01 (International)
(303) 938-1214 (fax)
society@newmessage.org
www.newmessage.org
www.alliesofhumanity.org
www.newknowledgelibrary.org

Connect with us:

www.youtube.com/TheNewMessageFromGod
www.facebook.com/NewMessageFromGod
www.facebook.com/MarshallSummers
www.twitter.com/GodsNewMessage

ABOUT THE WORLDWIDE COMMUNITY OF THE NEW MESSAGE FROM GOD

The New Message from God is being shared by people around the world. Representing more than 90 countries and over 20 languages, a worldwide community of students has formed to receive and study the New Message and to support the mission of the Messenger and The Society.

Learn more about the worldwide community of people who are learning and living the New Message from God and taking the Steps to Knowledge towards a new and inspired life.

Become a part of a worldwide community of people who are pioneering a new chapter in the human experience. The New Message has the power to awaken the sleeping brilliance in people everywhere and bring new inspiration and wisdom into the lives of people from all nations and faith traditions.

Hear the Voice of Revelation speaking directly
on the purpose and importance of the Worldwide Community:
www.newmessage.org/theworldwidecommunity

Learn more about the educational opportunities available in the
Worldwide Community:

Forum - www.newmessage.org/forum
Free School - www.newmessage.org/school
Live Internet Broadcasts and International Events -
www.newmessage.org/events
Annual Encampment - www.newmessage.org/encampment
Online Library and Study Pathway - www.newmessage.org/experience

BOOKS OF THE NEW MESSAGE FROM GOD

God Has Spoken Again

The One God

The New Messenger

The Greater Community

Greater Community Spirituality

Steps to Knowledge

Relationships & Higher Purpose

Living The Way of Knowledge

Life in the Universe

The Great Waves of Change

Wisdom from the Greater Community I & II

Secrets of Heaven

Read the books of the New Message online at
www.newmessage.org/library